I0147421

The Promise of Living

Also by GEORGE A. GOENS

Letters on the Promise of Living

Resilient Leadership for Turbulent Times

Soft Leadership for Hard Times

Mastering School Reform

Getting the Most from Public Schools

The Promise of Living

• • • • • • •

Loss, Life, and Living

GEORGE A. GOENS

TURNING
STONE
PRESS

First published in 2013 by Turning Stone Press, an imprint
of Red Wheel/Weiser, LLC
With offices at:
665 Third Street, Suite 400
San Francisco, CA 94107
www.redwheelweiser.com

Copyright © 2013 by George A. Goens
All rights reserved. No part of this publication may be
reproduced or transmitted in any form or by any means,
electronic or mechanical, including photocopying, recording, or by any information storage and retrieval system,
without permission in writing from Red Wheel/Weiser,
LLC. Reviewers may quote brief passages.

ISBN: 978-1-61852-052-4

Cover design by Jim Warner

Printed in the United States of America
10 9 8 7 6 5 4 3 2 1

For . . .

The families and children who live with a loss from a maternal death

Curtis, a great son and loving father for Julia and Eddie

Bill and Adam, my sons-in-law, who provide love and care for my other grandchildren

Claire and Luke who bring me joy

and

Betsy who continues to live in my heart

Contents

I will not let disappointments or unhappiness overwhelm me. I will accept that things do go wrong but also look ahead to what I can make right.

—Betsy Bower, 1990, Class Essay

Introduction

L ife, complete with unexpected turns and shifts, cre-ates surprising twists and contradictions. We can pre-pare for it, but we cannot control the seemingly constant state of disequilibrium that sometimes borders on chaos. Nothing is ever static. Things are always in flux, some-times very subtly, and at other times with unexpected power and swiftness.

Inexplicable events happen in life, many contrary to our belief in the natural order. Our rational plans and sense of equilibrium are upset. Chaos seems to reign in both our internal and external worlds.

Ups and downs and gains and losses occur sometimes simultaneously. Our plateau of certainty evaporates and the terrain transforms into peaks of joy and valleys of loss. Metaphorically, there are times when we glide gen-tly through life and at other times we crash into painful circumstances—some small and others overwhelmingly deep and difficult.

Sometimes good fortune shines on us simply because we happen to be in the right spot at the right time. Through seemingly serendipitous events, we meet our lifetime partner in an unexpected place at an unplanned time. But then there is the difficult twist of fate, and we face a health emergency, an errant driver crashes into us, or a family member dies suddenly. In an instant, we can fall into the darkness of loss without warning or reason.

All losses, however, are not the same. Some we expect. Growing old and letting go of youth is one. We understand each phase of life from childhood to old age and foresee it for ourselves. Other losses we determine and accept. At some point or another we realize we are not going to play professional hockey, be a ballerina, or become a jazz musician. Letting go of childhood dreams is a part of maturing, and as we reach middle age, we adapt to activities that are in harmony with the changes of our body, metabolism, and wisdom.

Death is the ultimate loss. It is absolute. But all deaths are not the same. The death of a loved one raises fear—of a cloudy future, of how we are going to get along, and of not being able to find that safe harbor of unconditional love that we need to thrive.

The death of a child, regardless of his or her age however, has a unique, devastating power all its own. The very essence and spirit of our lives change: relationships, dreams, hopes, connections, perceptions, values, beliefs.

Loss fused with fear can cement us to the past, looking into the rear view mirror of life, searching for comfort, and dreaming of what might have been. Facing "what is" becomes daunting and uncertain. Anger and sadness can freeze us in place. The energy we need to live our own lives evaporates because death steals the future.

In these most difficult of times, we can lose the drive and spirit to live as we numbly walk through each day with our hearts fractured and souls deadened. For some, the will to live and carry on diminishes and the mind becomes non-rational. We dwell on the devastation this death causes and fantasize about a future that never will be realized. We hope to wake from a dark dream, and we make magical deals with God trying to barter our lives for the return of our daughter or son. But no deal is possible.

The question is, what will we do when we face inevitable losses and death? This book is the story of an ordinary life filled with some successes and failures and quaked by stark losses. A formidable challenge for all of us is how we move ahead with our lives, fulfill our destiny, and find happiness and wholeness again, all while honoring those we loved so deeply who died.

We must face losses alone in the quiet of our hearts and souls, while living in a community with family and friends—no easy task and one immune to clichés and glib platitudes.

Good-byes

To say good-bye is to live.

We learn from our first breath

To the time of holy departure

The impermanence of everything

Except saying good-bye

Good-byes come with ashen faces

Or dressed in the winds of time

Good-byes swim in the well of love

And drop as tears from the eyes of sadness

Good-byes live in the noble castle of hope

Or walk the stony path of loneliness

Good-byes fly on the wings of opportunity
And tumble on the corners of dice

Age teaches us youth's delicateness,
Love discovers hidden valleys of the heart,
Time spins like falling leaves, and
Fear fractures the spirit and will

The good-byes we experience
Show in the lines of time
Sculpted on our faces
And live forever seared in our soul

The poetry, good, bad, or indifferent, is mine unless stated otherwise. These poems are reflections of my feelings and disposition at the time they were written.

When my daughter died, I wrestled with the beliefs and principles I learned throughout my life about happiness, living, religion, purpose, and meaning. Inevitably, it seems, I went through a quiet metamorphosis about these things. In the poetry, my views on "God," for example, may not be consistent as my feelings or perceptions changed with events. They are presented in the text because that is what I thought at that time. My religious beliefs and principles were challenged as I moved through my individual journey in coming to peace with the death of my daughter, and I am still challenging and working to resolve my beliefs to this day.

≈ 1 ≈

March 9th

There is no tragedy in life like the death of a child. Things never get back to the way they were.

—Dwight David Eisenhower

March 9th was going to be a great day; in fact, it was to be a bellwether day that we would remember and celebrate for years to come. My first grandson was finally arriving. He did arrive, but with an unexpected turn to the other side of life's spectrum.

Some days come in softly, caressed in an aura of love and optimism. That's the kind of day it was supposed to be. But it mutated into a surreal clash of life and death and joy and grief in a matter of hours.

Intense moments like this scorch themselves into our very being. They burn themselves into our psyche and memory and are resurrected by the simple, mundane ringing of a telephone or the flair of a spoken phrase. March 9, 2004, is a day that lives with me every day without exception.

The day before was filled with anticipation and excitement tinged with curiosity. Luke was going to be born. We knew the baby was a boy because Betsy and Bill found out from the doctor via the marvels of modern medicine. I wondered what he would look like and, over the long term, what kind of person he would be. Quite an occasion, I thought—my first grandson.

On the morning of the 9th, I met with my business partner, Lou, who proves that a guy can find a best friend after the age of 55. We discussed where we were with a client contract. After two and a half hours of planning and kibitzing, I decided to head home because, as I told Lou, "Today I'm going to be a grandfather for the second time!"

Lou and I laughed and he wished me well. "Congratulations, pal," he said, "It's a great day for you. I can't wait until I'm a grandfather."

"You know, Lou, there's nothing like it," I added. "Joy, complete joy."

While driving the 40 minutes back to my place, I thought about my granddaughter, Claire, and how excited she was to have a baby brother. As a four-year-old, she had a puckish sense of humor. When asked what she wanted to name her new baby brother, she replied "Spot," and then let out a hearty laugh.

Betsy went to the hospital early that morning to be induced. I expected a call when I got home, but when I looked at the answering machine—no word. I didn't think anything was unusual and figured the call would come soon: after all, some births take time.

I worked through that afternoon and expected my son, Curtis, to call. He and his wife, Jennie, were visiting Betsy in Florida to spend some time with her and also to help out with the baby. Late afternoon bled into early evening, and a subtle sense of uncertainty was beginning to slowly creep into my consciousness. Babies function on their own schedule, I thought. Time really doesn't exist for them. I checked my phone every 15 minutes and tried to call Curtis but to no avail. Finally, he called me and simply said, "The birth is going slow. I'll call you as soon as I know something."

That call broke the deafening afternoon silence and provided a bit of relief from the leaden ambiguity I was feeling. However, thinking about Betsy struggling with labor caused an aching concern that began to darken my mind. It was over eight hours, but I remember women telling stories of births that were real marathons.

The tempo of my impatience increased, raising a quiet fear of separation. What could be taking so long? Then, at about 5:30 p.m., the phone rang. I dashed to pick it up. It was Peter, my neighbor, who asked me to go to a movie, *The Fog of War*, because his wife was not interested. I told him I had to get out of the house, "I'm getting stir crazy waiting for a call from Florida about the birth of my grandson. A two-hour movie may get my mind off things."

We got back at 9:30 p.m. and met Eileen, Peter's wife, in the driveway. I told her that Betsy was in a long labor and that I was getting a bit concerned. Always a positive person, she replied, "There's probably a call on your answering machine now telling you that your grandson has arrived."

"Yeah . . . yeah, you're probably right," I replied, hoping she was.

I hustled into the house expecting to see a flashing light on the answering machine. Nothing! I didn't know what to think. The anxiety intensified, and helplessness swelled in my chest—a condition that was strange to me. I always believed I was "response-able"; capable of reacting to situations. I always felt that I could do something in most any circumstance. I hoped whoever came up with the phrase, "no news is good news," knew what he was talking about.

I called, but still couldn't reach Curtis. My sense of detachment was troubling and growing arduous. I felt frustrated and impotent. My rational side thought, she's in the hospital with good doctors and giving birth takes time. I recollected stories of long deliveries from friends and thought, Betsy's going to have a real tale to tell when this is over.

I sat in my leather chair, flipping through golf and news magazines and watching CNN. Waiting. Occasionally I put my head back and rested my eyes as the minutes dragged by slowly. I looked at the clock. I called Curtis again. No answer. Anxiety was evolving into anger at being snubbed. It was 11:20 p.m. I took my cell phone to bed with me, and I made sure the house phone ringer was on high volume; I didn't want to sleep through the call, if I was able to sleep at all.

In bed, I was unsettled; a flood of thoughts rushed through my mind. My eyes were wide open. I bunched up my pillow and turned on my side to look out the window at the full moon. I stared at the moonlight reflecting on the utility shed across the driveway. The light glistened off the golden shooting star weathervane at the peak of the shed's roof. I hoped it was a positive omen that everything was all right.

Feeling out of the loop, I thought, maybe they are all exhausted and will call first thing in the morning. Fear produced restlessness that agitated mind and body. Even though I'm not a religious person, I said a prayer for Betsy and my grandson, Luke. In troubling times, I guess even people like me who have not been in a church for years might have a prayer drop from their lips. Maybe even the prayers of heathens are heard and answered, I thought. Eventually, I fell into a light, fitful sleep.

The ringing phone shocked me totally awake out of my sleep. It was 3:52 a.m. When I think of that day, I can still see those illuminated digits on the clock. I jumped to my feet, rushed to my office, turned on the light, and answered the call breathing heavily from the dash to the phone.

"Dad, you have to get down here right away. Betsy's in trouble," Curtis's voice wavered as he shouted into the phone.

"What?" Stunned, I could hear his words but I didn't understand as disbelief and panic began to explode in my mind. "What?"

"Just get down here as soon as you can!"

"Is she okay? Is she okay? Alive?" Fear overwhelmed me. How could this happen? What's happening?

"It's bad, Dad. You can't wait. She may not make it." Curtis's voice cracked and the intensity of the moment struck me like a bullet in my chest. My body shook uncontrollably.

I hung up, totally disoriented, my heart pounding, and literally walked in circles from room to room, panicked and not knowing what to do. I yelled to myself, "Hang on Betsy . . . hang on! Fight! Don't die. Don't die!" as if she could feel my words across the miles. Somehow, in my haze I called my neighbor Peter to let him know that I had to catch a plane to Florida because Betsy was having difficulty with the birth. I needed help.

Panic and confusion took over. I had felt this state once before. When I was a school superintendent in the Midwest, one of my associate principals was shot to death in the hallway while school was in session. Not knowing if the perpetrator was still in the building, we were locked down for three hours. In crisis, sequences get confused, I forgot some details, and remember others starkly. This time, however, the shock struck me so much harder; I felt my chest tightening as I felt my personal world dissolving. My body and my legs were weak and shaky. The emotion was blinding.

Somehow Peter or Eileen called the airlines and got me a 6:15 a.m. flight to Fort Myers, Florida. I shot through downtown without regard for stop signs or traffic lights. I called Jennie, my heart pounding, and my fingers tightly gripping the steering wheel as I flew down the highway.

"Jennie, what's happening?"

"I'm not sure," she said.

"Tell me the truth, God dammit! Is she alive?" I yelled into the phone.

"I don't know . . . I really don't know," she said, her voice quivering.

"I've got to know! I just can't fly the two and half hours to Florida wondering if my daughter's alive. She's my daughter . . . she's my daughter, I've got to know!" I said, "Just find out and have Curtis call me." I hung up and hit the accelerator.

About a mile and a half from the airport Curtis called. His voice betrayed the message before the words came. "Betsy died, Dad. Get here right away." He broke down in tears.

Stunned and speechless, I stammered, "I'm on my way. I got a 6:15 flight. What about the baby?"

"He's OK. He's OK. Just hurry."

I hung up and bolted through the stoplight, crying out at the top of my lungs, "NO!!!!!! NO!!!!!" Every time I'm on that road, the rush of memories and feelings bubble up and my heart pounds. Those feelings are chiseled in my soul and bones.

I rushed to the airport at breakneck speed, got to the ticket counter and told the agent to upgrade my one-way ticket to Fort Myers to first class regardless of the expense. The thought of being at the back of the airplane, standing in line, waiting to disembark was excruciating.

I headed for the TSA inspection line. I carried no luggage, just my sport coat and personal effects. I showed the TSA inspector my "official government-issued photo ID," passed through the checkpoint, and headed for the inspection line, took off my shoes, my sport coat, and walked through the metal detector doorframe. As my shoes and sport coat came through the x-ray machine, a TSA agent said, "Are these your shoes and sport coat?" I looked at my watch. It was 5:37 a.m.

"Yes," I said assertively. "I have to catch the 6:15 flight to Fort Myers."

"Can I see your boarding pass, please," the agent stated authoritatively. "A one-way ticket?"

"Yes, I have to catch this flight to Florida."

"May I see your wallet?" I looked at my watch again to see the minutes ticking by, and fears began to overtake me that I could miss the plane. I couldn't fathom spending hours sitting at the airport while my daughter lay dead in Fort Myers.

"Yes, but make it quick! I have to catch this flight!" I barked. "I have a family emergency."

"Well, you should have gotten here two hours ahead of your flight," the inspector said. "Then you wouldn't have to worry about catching the plane." He started picking through my wallet . . . credit cards, receipts, insurance cards . . . one by one. I thought I was going to explode.

I physically reacted and took a step toward him and said in a demanding, hoarse voice. "Two hours ago, I didn't know my daughter had died. GET ME THROUGH THIS DAMN LINE!" I commanded.

"Just be careful what you're saying," he warned, "if you want to get on that plane."

"Just hurry up. I must catch this flight!"

He looked at my ID, compared it to the ticket, examined my shoes, and inspected my sport coat. After what seemed like an eternity, he handed my ticket back.

I put my shoes and coat on, turned, and said to him, "If I miss my flight, I'm going to come back and find you!"

I ran to the gate. The airline agent welcomed me and told me to quickly get on board. I took my aisle seat in row 1 next to a well-coiffed, blonde, middle-aged woman. I sat trying to catch my breath and compose myself when a curious numbness came over me as I saw my world explode in disbelief. How could this happen? I thought.

I was angry and couldn't understand why; if there was a God at all, how he could he have a mother die at the time she was giving birth to a child? "What the fuck kind of God is that?" I thought. Betsy had been studying the Bible and seemingly coming to terms with religion. What irony, I thought, reading about a merciful, loving God and then dying without ever seeing your son. What a sick joke!

Like any parent, I would have given my life in exchange for Betsy's. I felt I had lived life, experienced highs and some devastating lows, had given it a shot and could leave without regret. What more could I contribute? I thought to myself. Betsy only lived 34 years and she certainly had greater responsibilities raising two young children. To this day, I still wish I could make that exchange. But magical thinking is just that—a delusion.

The well-coiffed and neatly dressed woman in the seat next to me broke my emotional trance and asked, "Are you going to Florida on business or pleasure?"

"Neither. Unfortunately, this is a sad trip." I hesitated a moment to say more. Then I turned to her and said, "My daughter died this morning giving birth to my grandson." In that conversation and moment, Betsy's death became a part of my new reality—that she was gone, just like that, in a blink.

She looked at me and said what most people say, "Oh, I'm so sorry." There was an awkward moment of silence between us and then she confided in a quiet voice, "I lost my son two years ago. He was only 22 years old when he became seriously ill. I am so, so sorry about your daughter. People just don't realize the impact of losing a child—no matter at what age."

I was stunned, but in a strange way, the compassion in her voice and the look in her green eyes provided me with a brief moment of solace that someone understood the beginning of the journey I was taking. We had an instantaneous connection and we spoke about our dead children as we flew above the clouds. I thought, "What are the chances that I would sit next to another parent who suffered the death of a child?" It was almost mystical. She gave me some sense of comfort in that panic-filled flight, because her story was not unlike mine. She understood my pain and sensed the frantic nature of my flight to Florida and the heaviness I felt.

She asked if I had a place to stay while I was there and said that I could stay with her and her husband because they had a large house on Sanibel Island. I thanked her and

said that I appreciated her kindness but that I had arrange-
ments with my family. Her sincere presence and her compassion helped calm my panicked soul. She knew . . . and
sat by me through the miles, a stranger, being there, with
an understanding soul.

The Weight

Sometimes you have to be buried in the solitude of your
grief . . . Alone. Without others . . . to feel the intense pain
of loss and isolation from those you love so deeply. Only
then . . . only then can the sadness of loss become the
agent of true change. There are no words others can say
to lift the weight of death.

We landed and I thanked her and flew out the door. I
dashed through the airport to the exit. Jennie was waiting
for me and we drove most of the way to the hospital in
subdued thought, skipping the usual small talk about the
flight and the doings of our lives. I was oblivious to traffic,
street signs, or highways. I can't remember much of the
limited conversation we did have. I think we talked about
who was at the hospital, the time that Betsy died, how
Luke was, and how Bill was coping. I asked if my former
wife, Mary, had arrived. But overall, silence was our companion: my mind was buried in pounding disbelief.

I remember the left turn we took at a stoplight where
I first saw the hospital, which was a smaller satellite facility for "minor" surgeries and procedures. What an irony,
I thought, a facility for routine medical procedures. Were
they equipped for life and death issues?

We parked the car and I hurried into the hospital, Jennie trailing behind, where I saw Curtis at the elevator. We hugged tightly and Curtis's voice cracked as we talked. I saw Mary for the first time in years and we embraced, bonded by love, but this time by a mutual love for our daughter. Any differences we had had in the past disintegrated in the burning sorrow of Betsy's death. Mary looked ashen and exhausted, her big brown eyes sunken and dim. She looked smaller and more fragile than the last time I saw her.

We went to the room the hospital provided for the family, and three of Betsy's friends were there helping with Luke and consoling Bill. I wanted to see my grandson, and I felt a twinge of discomfort and frustration because of the chatter and the crowded room. I needed quiet, space, and privacy. I wanted the friends to leave so I could hold Luke and sit with Bill, Mary, and Curtis. Bill's mom and dad were taking care of Claire at home, who, at that time, was not yet aware that her mother was not ever going to come home again.

My bones ached as I looked into Luke's little face. What a surrealistic moment: the confluence of life and death occurring simultaneously. He was totally unaware that his life was different, almost from the time of birth, because he was motherless within an hour of his arrival. I thought of Claire and the incomprehensible loss she was about to experience.

At times, I didn't know how to feel. Holding Luke close, I felt a deep sense of subdued joy tinged with sadness for him and Claire. I vowed to ensure that he would find happiness and meaning in life and not feel as I did as a four-year-old child after the death of my father. I always felt different from other children and I was fearful that something would happen to my mother, leaving me alone and abandoned. Insecurity was a companion of mine, along with a fear of being abandoned—rejected.

The hospital administrator came in and asked if there was anything more that he could do. He said they would do anything to make us comfortable at "this difficult time." I stared at the tray of sandwiches and the soft drinks sitting on the table. My natural skepticism toward large organizations made me think that the hospital would do anything now to avoid any type of lawsuit or legal action having to do with the death of a woman giving birth in their facility, particularly, when there was no prior indication of any problem with the pregnancy or birth.

Sandwiches, I thought, were no solace. Although I was numb about the events, a part of my mind veered off, rationally, to finding out what happened and whose responsibility it was. I wanted to get all of the facts. I was always good in those moments of profound crisis and maintained a very logical edge because I knew about legal matters and lawsuits from my past professional experience. My cynical point of view, in part, was the child of the anger and disbelief I was feeling.

The administrator said that we could go to the intensive care unit to see Betsy before they performed an autopsy to find out what had transpired in the last 12 hours. I wasn't certain I wanted to see Betsy in the ICU. The tension built in my stomach as we all went down the antiseptic-smelling elevator to the first floor. No one said a word, even though we were all feeling the same pain— we just all stared at the bland stainless steel door.

When I walked in the room filled with medical equipment, medicine stands, and a surgical-type light, I saw her. Her body didn't seem like Betsy's. The truth of the situation hit me hard as tangible reality struck home. There she was—her lifeless body looked like a facsimile of my daughter, not the real thing. Something was missing.

Her hair, which was flowing over the pillow, was longer than when I saw her last. She had a breathing tube coming out from her mouth that had little scuffs of blood around it. She looked so different to me. Vacant.

Her spirit was gone and the body no longer looked like the person I remembered. Her face was void of all the life force and vigor that she put into everything she did. Her lifeless, expressionless face, still beautiful, almost looked like a wax replica of who she was. I guess the human spirit, while intangible, fills our body with distinctive energy. When it is gone, the dead body becomes an empty receptacle of who we were, devoid of our character and vitality.

Betsy's uniqueness was gone, although her body remained. I realized then the beauty and vigor of the human spirit. Maybe scientists are right when they profess that the universe is made of strings of energy. If that is the case, I hope that her energy will live in Luke and Claire and will live on scattered throughout the universe.

Betsy's death had so many dimensions to it, not only for Mary and me as parents, and Bill as a husband, but also for her children. Little Claire was at home, unaware of the day's heartbreaking events. Sometime in the early evening, Bill said that he had to talk to Claire and let her know what was happening. Mary and I went along with him. It was around 7:30 p.m. Claire was already in bed. The stairway leading to her second-floor bedroom was dark and the house was quiet and still. Bill said that he wanted to tell Claire by himself.

Mary and I stood on the stairway as we heard him whisper to her that "Mommy died" and was not going to come home. That "she is in heaven." To this day, I can feel that moment in the pit of my stomach and I can still hear Claire's soft anguished sob and cry. The impact of Betsy's death became clearest in Claire's small, almost squeaky whimper. The deep sorrow of a child was overwhelming. Claire didn't totally understand, and I'm sure she didn't know what or where "heaven" was. It was simply up there, in the sky.

Claire and Betsy were two peas in a pod. The joy in Claire's eyes when she was with her mother is something I will never forget seeing and it is reflected in the many photographs that I saved. Betsy loved Claire so very deeply and took great delight in being a mother. Together, they epitomized love and harmony—parent and child. Claire was looking forward to little Luke and Betsy had told her how much fun she would have with her little brother.

Death is such an abstraction to young children. We tell them that their mother "is in heaven," and they think of angels, clouds, and "up there" as they point to the sky. They don't really know that death is permanent and that things will never be as they were. As a child, I experienced this same grief and fright. Only in retrospect do I realize the crushing impact of a parent's death on a child. What went on in Claire's mind was hard for me to imagine, even though I experienced it myself. I just thought my dad had disappeared.

When Claire saw Luke for the first time at the hospital, a sweet smile broke on her face as she held her little brother, while Mary cuddled them both. Simultaneously losing a mother and gaining a brother must have been confusing to her. Her resilience and fortitude then and now are truly astonishing and heroic to me. I feel a deep connection to her, my first grandchild, and also to Luke, who through the innocence of infancy was totally unaware of what occurred and that life as we know it changed in an instant.

Mary and I stayed with Bill at the house and Curtis and Jennie went to a small, family-run motel. I slept on the downstairs couch, and Mary stayed in the room with Claire. Claire and Mary were very close. The physical resemblance of Claire to her grandmother was uncanny. Everyone who saw them together knew they were related, and some thought Mary was Claire's mother. Both have beautiful, big brown eyes and wonderful, enchanting smiles.

Exhausted, I lay on the couch and the gray moonlight shone through the sliding doors of the lanai. The pounding thud of death finally cracked opened my emotions and I broke down, crying and sobbing without control, saying, "Betsy, Betsy, Betsy." Death's grim truth struck and the grief was unbearable, just pouring out of me. I thought of the last conversation I had had with her, and of her upbeat enthusiasm about Luke's birth. I was so glad that my last words to her the day before she went to the hospital were, "I love you, Betsy."

Mary heard me crying downstairs and she came down and asked if I was all right. For the first time in years we held each other—joined by our profound sorrow and the shock of disbelief. The loss dispelled any anger or disillusionment that had accumulated between us over the years. We weren't ex-husband and ex-wife. We were just grief-stricken parents with broken hearts, clinging together in a flood of grief, trying to comprehend the incomprehensible worst fear of parents.

On March 10th, the whole family walked in a daze. Bill, Curtis, and I picked out a casket, we went to Barnes

& Noble to get a copy of "Simple Gifts," the Shaker hymn that was a favorite of Betsy's that we wanted played at the church service. Then all of us flipped through hundreds of pictures of Betsy to include in the ceremony. It was a strange day: people were together but locked in their own fog of loss and grief. Other family members were making plans to gather in Florida from Wisconsin, Illinois, and Indiana for the church service on March 12th. The minister also visited and made the obligatory gestures to try to help us deal with the circumstances—a prayer and words about God's will and love—and then we discussed the components of the service.

The church service included eulogies from Bill, Mary, and me. I wanted words to portray Betsy as a person, what she stood for and what gave her life meaning. I summed up her eulogy by saying:

> The light within her served as a beacon of warmth for others and it also guided her on her journey through a principled life of meaning.
>
> • She sought out people everywhere she went—from Oconomowoc, to Madison, to Europe, to Birmingham, to Florida—she made great and lasting friendships.
>
> • She sought out goodness and saw God's humanness in all people, regardless of their standing in life. She befriended those without friends and reached out to others, developing deep relationships. Goodness—respect, kindness, empathy, acceptance, and understanding—always marked her relationships. She had a great hearty laugh, a keen sense of humor, and a wonderful smile.

- She learned life's hardest lesson—the ability to forgive. I am the biggest recipient of her forgiveness here today. And for that, Betsy, I am so deeply, deeply grateful.

- Finally, she sought to be a loving, nurturing, and compassionate wife and mother. We love Bill, her husband, very much, and we profoundly cherish Claire and little Luke, Betsy's last gift to us all—for they are the greatest and most lasting reminders of Betsy's spirit and goodness. She loved her family so totally and intensely.

Curtis was not going to speak at the funeral service. He was not as gregarious as his sister and was somewhat shy about speaking in front of a group. But after Mary gave her touching and moving comments, Curtis whispered to me if I thought he should say something. He hadn't prepared a written text.

I said, "Sure, this is the only moment you will have. Just relax and say what's in your heart."

His heartfelt impromptu comments about the importance of his sister in his life were the best of the eulogies— simple, clear, and loving. Spontaneous emotion and love are powerful. His sincere tribute still rests in my heart for its genuine tenderness. We then showed a slide presentation with pictures of the phases of Betsy's life—her smile radiated through most of them.

Religious platitudes do not give me much comfort at all—God's love, God's will, and God's plan always fall short. It is more fairy tale to me than any mystical grounding. However, the ritual of people coming together in a community and sharing common connections to honor Betsy's life was somewhat consoling.

I was never one for funeral services, but they do have two virtues: they give people the ability to demonstrate respect for the person's life, passion, and achievements; and they give people the opportunity to express their feelings. For me, it was touching and gratifying to see the impact of Betsy's life on others. She never achieved fame or great fortune, but those intangible things in life— respect, friendship, honor, compassion—meant so much to the people she touched. Although she was gone, her character remained.

As I looked at her broken family, I had nothing but compassion for Bill, Claire, and Luke. But fear whispered softly in my mind. I was worried about losing contact with my grandchildren. I'd heard stories of that happening and, while there is geographical distance between us, I did not want emotional or relationship distance to develop with the kids because Betsy was gone. I think the fear of losing those connections related to the feeling of isolation I had, at times, from growing up fatherless. This fear brought with it an intense obligation to remain a part of the kids' lives and to help Bill raise them in a positive and supportive manner.

Death sometimes walks in the velvet slippers of compassion, but at times, it marches in the hobnail boots of tragedy. Unexpected and chaotic events occur far from our ability to control or understand them. Although we all would like to live lives of consistent happiness, death emphasizes the fact that we do not control much. Our lives are not flat plateaus of happiness. Although we do experience the mountaintop of success, achievement, and joy, we also are going to experience the dark valley of sorrow and loss. March 9th was the epitome of crushing sorrow—a sorrow so deep that it flushed away everything else in my life.

One Day

One last day
the same number of minutes and
seconds ticking in the familiar rhythm,
living them as if there will be
another tomorrow with time
being our stable friend.

But one day, some day,
our last day will come,
slipping into our lives
on the invisible and deadly mists of destiny,
capping our time in a finite hourglass.

One last day lives with me
month after month, year after year
branded into my soul
and burned into my heart
by the clock that stopped
the ninth day of March.

⁓ 2 ⁓

Is Your Heart Heaven?

*When you are sorrowful, look again in your heart, and you
shall see that in truth you are weeping for that which has
been your delight.*

—Kahlil Gibran

The Christmas after Betsy died Claire and I had a quiet
moment sitting on the bed away from holiday deco-
rations and conversational buzz. Just the two of us. The
solitude of the bedroom was silent and soft. The whole
family was together at Mary's house to support each other
during the first major holiday after Betsy's death—one of
her favorite times of the year.

Claire looked up at me and asked, "Grandpa, where
is your dad?"

I was surprised at the question because we had never
talked about my father before.

"Well Claire," I said, "my dad died when I was four
years old."

She paused a moment, leaned toward me, and whispered, "Oh, Grandpa, you're just like me."

I gave her a soft hug and responded, "Yes, Claire, we
are a bit alike, aren't we."

We were linked not only by blood, but also by the tragic loss of a parent at the age of four—different generations experiencing the same loss, at the same age, 60 years apart.

She looked at me and then said, "You know, Grandpa, your wishes don't come true."

I looked at her innocent face and I could see bewilderment and pain.

"Why do you say that?"

"I wish I could grow wings so I could fly into the sky," she replied. "I would like to fly way up into the clouds."

I realized she had been grieving for her mother just as the rest of us were that holiday. We forget children feel the same sophisticated emotions we do, but with a genuine innocence that does not mask them. We were alike in another way also. I wanted to see her mother, too, and missed her desperately. Betsy's presence and energy were gone forever.

Dear Mommy

Dear Mommy,

I love you and miss you.
It hrts though.
But I noe it is Ok.
I wish you were back.

From,

Claire
Age 6

"Well, Claire, those kinds of wishes can't come true. When I was a little boy, I wished I could run fast like a horse through pastures and fields," I told her. "Although those kinds can't come true, many other wishes can." Then she asked another question—one that astounded me.

"Is your heart heaven?"

"Boy, that's a great question." I paused thinking about it and then said, "You know, it might be, Claire. Our hearts are filled with love and heaven is filled with love, too."

She then said, "I wish I could jump into a heart."

"Jump into a heart?"

"I just wish I could jump into my heart. . . ."

Her big brown eyes were soft with the sadness of wanting to see her mother again. I could feel her quiet pain of not understanding that death is forever and that she would not feel her mother's warm hugs and tenderness again.

I told her, "I wish I could see your Mom too, Claire. I miss her very, very much."

I choked up as we shared this heartfelt moment. My heart ached for her and I wished a wish that I couldn't deliver for her. I guess we all have impossible wishes, no matter what our age.

More than once, I heard adults tell her, " Oh, Claire, your mother will always live in your heart." or "Your mother went to heaven and is with God." She took that literally, which caused her to want to jump into her heart or to grow wings and fly up to heaven to visit her mother. This was a longing that could not be resolved, just accepted. If we could go, I would fly right next to her—we'd travel together to the other side.

Death is the dominant unyielding force in life. I really don't know about an afterlife or if heaven even exists, but her metaphor for heaven, in its innocent way, was more appropriate than others from ministers and other adults. Children have an innate unadulterated wisdom about them.

Who knows? Maybe Claire is right. Maybe our hearts are a piece of heaven. If so, then I know her heart and mine will eventually find peace and heal.

But the loss will always exist. The loss of a parent is a loss that lasts forever, one we feel and experience throughout our lives. The pain and anguish associated with it in our early years is overwhelmingly powerful. It is a seminal event that shapes our lives and relationships, and affects our personalities, desires, insecurities, and anxieties.

I remember that when my father died, I really didn't know where he had gone. I recall the night he died with the emergency lights and policemen. But all I knew was that I felt different because other kids had a father at home and I didn't. I didn't like that feeling. So when I look at my grandchildren, I feel intensely connected and want them not to feel "different"—not to feel a constant absence or void. No one can really replace a parent: not mentors, aunts, uncles, or role models. While all of them are important, they still are not Mom or Dad.

In a twist of fate, learning to live without Betsy united Claire and me. In my case, it was the loss of a daughter and the newly rekindled father-daughter relationship with Betsy. Claire lost her mother, the person she relied on for unconditional love, security, nurturing, and comfort. For both of us, these were deep, deep losses.

When I was with Claire, listening to her and dealing with my own feelings of loss, grief, and helplessness, I thought about the course of life and the fact that loss is an integral part of it. But not all losses are created equal.

Some are natural and normal, and others are overwhelming—causing life-long impact, both tangible and subtle.

Parents are supposed to die before us, usually as they move into old age, because that's the natural order. The loss of a child or the death of a parent at a very young age assaults our idea of normalcy. These losses are extraordinary and are out of sync with nature. They raise the specter of "Why me?" victimhood. Pain and anger can do that.

Certainly there are other losses in life. Many of them are just accepted as the typical path of life. As we grow older, we give up our youthful, fanciful dreams. There was a time when I realized I wasn't going to play left wing for the Chicago Blackhawks. This childhood dream evaporated once I grasped that while I was a very good hockey player, I just wasn't exceptional enough to make a living playing it.

We give up dreams as we learn to better understand ourselves from the disappointments and triumphs of experience. Reflecting on who we are, what we want to do with our lives, and using a healthy dose of realistic appraisal of our abilities can be very constructive for our future. Giving up those dreams actually may cause other opportunities to surface and shape us.

Some losses are self-inflicted—personal decisions we make that are destructive to others and ourselves. There are times we don't fully understand our own actions. I made one such decision that destroyed my marriage, changed my career, and resulted in my "first" loss of Betsy. The loss of my professional "calling" and the inability to pursue a noble cause and to apply my knowledge and skills were extremely tough, but losing this was not as hard as becoming estranged from my daughter. Certainly, destroying my reputation generated pain, self-anger, and guilt. Getting past these feelings and periods of regret and sorrow was not easy. But losing a job is not necessarily permanent and final; we can be restored, "whole," in another venue or role. Restoring relationships is much more difficult.

My decisions and my subsequent firing resulted in a difficult divorce and alienation from Betsy. She and I did not see each other for five years. During this estrangement, we had very little communication. I would send her notes periodically and letters on birthdays and holidays. The response was deadening silence—an extremely punishing non-response of indifference.

Indifference has a power that penetrates hearts beyond any other assault. As Elie Wiesel stated: "The opposite of love is not hate, it's indifference . . . the opposite of life is not death, it's indifference."

When I tried calling, the calls would sometimes end up with Betsy making brash and brutal comments that targeted my character directly. Once, in a very brief phone conversation right after the divorce, she angrily called me a scumbag. The pain that word caused was brutalizing and ripping. While she was in college, she had told me how much she admired me. And then, all of a sudden, I was reduced to the level of scumbag. That conversation was the beginning of our relationship disintegrating into no response to notes, cards, and letters, and the heart crushing hang-ups on my phone calls. I lost her in the maze of divorce and my self-centered, ego-driven fantasy.

All through her life, Betsy had strong principles and beliefs. She questioned authority—usually for the right reasons. I always told my kids to stand up for their principles and be the lone wolf howling in the wilderness, if necessary, while others sit silent in the face of injustice. I was proud of Betsy and Curtis when they did so.

Betsy's anger at me was based on principle. I disappointed her and betrayed the very principles I espoused. I lost credibility with all its damaging effects. My decisions were hurtful to the entire family and my role in the community. When people are seen in others' eyes as heroes, their fall from grace is hard and brutalizing, and the resulting disappointment plays out in harsh ways. Forgiveness is an alien concept in those times.

In fact, Betsy was so angry about the divorce that I was not invited to her wedding. I was cut out of her life. Who escorted her down the aisle? I didn't know. My only daughter got married and I was exiled from her life on one of her most important and memorable days. I spent that punishing day on Cape Breton Island in Nova Scotia in an effort to distract myself from the idea of sitting home in quiet or drunken desperation. It didn't work on either front.

Tough times! I was angry with myself and feeling guilty for being out of Betsy's life. I watched the clock that day and imagined the events that were taking place. I still wonder how she felt on her wedding day. In my heart, I think the fact she played "Simple Gifts" at her wedding was significant. I love that Shaker hymn and shared it with her many times when she was a child. I even gave her a copy to listen to when she spent a year in France. Although I was not physically at her wedding, in some ways, I think I was.

After she was married, I kept calling and writing. Although Curtis was angry at me for the divorce, he said to his mother that I was still his father and he was going to have a relationship with me. That was a real blessing. At times, Curtis told me that Betsy would ask about me. He told her that if she was interested in what I was doing, she should call me. My relationship with my son helped rescue me from the ache of total isolation and rejection, and maybe other things as well.

I wrote in the journal I was keeping in 1998,

> Betsy, I am not whole without you. We are connected physically—my blood rushes through your veins and my genes inhabit your DNA. We are connected in mind and body and are part of the same fabric of life. Without contact, we are not complete: I know I live in your heart and soul. And you live in mine. Connection is natural and inevitable whether in this life or later. We are part of the same story.

The dull persistent ache of Betsy's repudiation wore on me. She treated me as if I was dead—gone, forgotten, a nonentity. After so much time passed, I told a friend some prophetic words I wish I could take back. I was fed up, angry, feeling sorry for myself. After futile years of trying to connect, I said, "I'm done with this. I could live my life without Betsy." How wrong I was! How naïve and stupid! How ignorant of the depth of the loving bond between father and daughter. The pain of indifference blunts the feeling we hold deep in our hearts.

I stopped writing or calling for some months. And then, on a warm early spring day in Vermont, I was working at home, looking out the window at the budding flowers and the goldfinches ravishing the bird feeder. It was just after Claire was born. I decided to make one last phone call to Betsy. I walked out on the deck and felt the warmth of the sun after a long, cold winter. I called, expecting the same response that I had gotten over the past years, but something happened.

I said, "Hi Betsy. It's Dad."

I waited a second and then she responded with, "What are you doing, Dad? Are you working?"

Her voice was missing the cold, sharp edge. For the first time in five years, I heard the word "Dad" from my daughter.

Stunned, I didn't know what to say. A few seconds of silence passed.

I expected an angry comment, but she followed with, "Are you working on a project or something?" I remembered that soft voice from the past when our conversations were familiar, easy, relaxed, and warm.

"Yeah . . . I'm working at home," I said cautiously. "I just got off the phone with my business partner, Lou. We have a contract I'm puttering with—writing some stuff."

I waited, and then it was just as if a fog lifted and we continued chattering like old times. At the end of the conversation, she invited me to come to Florida to see Claire for the first time. I hung up the phone, sat on the step of the deck, and bawled like a baby. I couldn't believe that I would see Betsy again after years of devastating silence and meet my first grandchild. And with that came a rebirth of our relationship, although it was a bit more nuanced than before.

Claire's birth was the mediating force, I think. Being with Betsy again, and her new family, made my life more complete—it was a godsend really. The hole of that five-year loss was deep and at times dark. But I never gave up hope of reconciling and being a father to her again; I wanted to stop being a memory.

One day on one of my visits when Betsy and I were driving to the grocery store, "What was happening with you? Why did you betray Mom?"

"I really don't know. It's a long story. Dealing with the murder and crisis when I was superintendent. . . . I was out of control. There's no defense for it. What I did wasn't right and I am deeply sorry. There really aren't any excuses for something like that," I replied softly. We always said that some day we would discuss what happened, but time ran out and we never did.

Being estranged all those years did not really prepare me for her death. This wasn't a legal proceeding like divorce between husband and wife, as difficult as that is. I always felt that someday Betsy and I would resolve issues and heal the hurt and sadness of the past. Death, however, erases any opportunity to reconcile events. Doors of opportunity are closed forever. When we are faced with the death of someone close to us, however, our lives take a different color and tone and cannot be restored to the same sense of wholeness that existed before.

Estrangement is not death because there is always the hope of seeing each other again in an aura of forgiveness. I'm so thankful for that call on that early spring day in Vermont. I can't fathom being barred from her life and then having her die before we could talk and reconcile. That weight surely would have broken me. I really couldn't live, in a complete sense, without being in Betsy's life.

Fear is our companion in loss. When I lost my job, I feared that I would never find another one, and this was in addition to coping with economic distress and wrestling with my own confusion and self-image. I lost friends as a result my personal actions and was apprehensive about my ability to develop other close and comfortable relationships.

I knew that as we age, we have to let friends go because they have to follow their own destiny, paths, and passions.

They are meant to be with us for a period of time and then they have to move on to other endeavors. We wish them well and cherish the moments that we had together.

Letting people go—even though they've been close friends, mentors, lovers, or confidants—is part of the course we travel in our life's journey. Everyone has to live and meet his or her destiny.

Betsy's death, however, was a more complicated configuration of feelings, relationships, and worries. At first I feared that I would not have any relationship or access to my grandchildren. I worried about them and their future. I wanted them to live happy lives filled with excitement and meaning, and I wanted them to bond and to take care of each other. And, having them remember their mother was so very important. I worried about my son-in-law, Bill, and how he was going to manage a family and find another relationship that would be nurturing and loving for him, Claire, and Luke.

Deep and constant sorrow accompanied these uncertainties. Friends encouraged me, "You can get through the sadness." Sadness cannot be avoided: it is just part of the package. The question for me was what should I do with the sorrow and loneliness that I experienced after Betsy died? I lived with loneliness and a sense of separation, but sorrow was causing me to recoil and shut down from life and its opportunities. Loving deeply and everlastingly brings vulnerability when death strikes.

Sorrow has other dimensions. It can also help us with our losses. While loneliness brings separation and solitude, that solitude coupled with deep reflection helped me in a strange way to find comfort from my feelings and a sense of peace. It helped me embrace my feelings and find stillness in the turmoil of death.

On the other hand, sorrow tempted me to shut down and build concrete walls of anger and bitterness, become self-absorbed and rigid, cling to what was and become irate about what had changed. I was clinging to the past and looking to the future with bitterness that could cut me off from other relationships and passions.

A Chinese proverb states, "You cannot prevent the birds of sorrow from flying overhead, but you can prevent them from building nests in your hair." I could feel the birds flying over my head looking for nesting places in the residue of anger and resentment that threatened to harden me and destroy any chance of finding harmony with my life again.

Sorrow opened me up, dissolving a bit of the go-it-alone, "buck up" attitude I had developed. I realized that I was not alone in my mourning and that others had felt the same deep darkness and sting of loss. Sorrow has a way of humanizing connections to others through empathy and kindness.

I can't answer Claire's question about hearts and heaven. I do know that the sadness of Betsy's death reached the deepest recesses of my heart. Without deep love, there would be no feeling of loss.

Loss opened my eyes to the meaninglessness of much of what we do and the emptiness of what we pursue. Living life is not about collecting titles, building bank accounts, or acquiring the luxuries of materialism. Brass rings are hollow. Those things are neither precious nor worthless. They are just things—of little consequence to a life of meaning and purpose.

When all is said and done, relationships and the love that is a part of them are what life is all about. Just like Claire, I yearn to see her mother again. I would give anything to have just one more hour with her sharing our time and love. Maybe from a philosophical standpoint, we grow into wisdom through experiencing and reflecting on the losses inherent in life.

Coping with loss taught me one other thing. If we love the person who died, then we have a responsibility to use that sorrow and loss to demonstrate love for others and find a new and just path in our life. In that way, I can honor Betsy and my love for her.

Is Your Heart Heaven?

"Is your heart heaven?"
You asked,
Your four-year-old dark eyes seeking
An answer from an aging man.

"Good question," I said,
Searching for an answer.

"What's in your heart, Claire?"
I asked.

"Love, Grandpa,"
You replied.

"Well, maybe our hearts are heaven,"
I said.
"Heaven is love."

"I wish," you said,
"That we could dive into my heart."

"Dive into a heart?"
I questioned.

"Yes. That's where my mom lives,"
You said.

I cried.

⪡ 3 ⪢

Remembering Forgotten Memories

*The bitterest tears shed over graves are for words left
unsaid and deeds left undone.*

—Harriet Beecher Stowe

When I was 37 years old, my five-year-old son Curtis
went with me to the cemetery where my father was
buried. Mary and Betsy were attending a bridal shower
close by, so I thought I would pay my respects to my
grandmother, father, and uncle.

I had worked cutting grass at that cemetery years
ago to get through college. I never was the type to visit
those gravesites regularly, however. I know some people
do. When I worked there, I could almost set my watch by
the arrival of a blue, two-door, 1954 Chevrolet that drove
through the cemetery on its solemn rounds around 11:50
a.m., just before our grass crew's lunch break. The guys
couldn't understand what that woman was doing every
day. Neither could I. Today, I have a better picture.

Working there was strange in a way. I learned that
even after death social standing and money seem to

matter. Money buys position, at least when it comes to the location of graves. Status seems to follow you to the grave. In addition, cemeteries have a pecking order in terms of gravesite care. The sections at the entrance—the ones with the large granite memorial stones—had the grass cut and groomed twice a week. The graves in the more modest sections, where my dad was buried, were groomed once a week or so. Actually, each time I cut on the "hill" where my dad and grandmother were buried, I gave their gravesites the premium treatment and extra care—at no cost.

The "pauper" section was only cut maybe once or twice a summer, when it was hot and the grass was slow growing and brown in the other sections. There, the markers were in disarray and the field grass was long. It was actually difficult to discern individual gravesites. No one visited these sites. Overgrown and barren, they were forgotten, along with those buried there.

The trip to my father's grave was different this time. Curtis and I walked up the hill and found his gravestone. I looked at the headstone. He lived a short 46 years, at the time just nine years older than I was.

I have fuzzy memories of the night he died. I remember seeing the red emergency lights circling the off-white living room walls while emergency personnel tended to my dad on the couch. Someone escorted me from the room and I hid under the dining room table. While I was sitting there where I used to play with my toys and out of sight, I distinctly remember studying the motorcycle policeman's black boots. I don't know why, but while I was under the table, I was aware of someone turning the switch on for the chandelier over the dining room table so they could get brighter light in the room. I guess we remember unusual things about significant days that affect the rest of our lives—short flickering, disjointed snippets of memory. What will Claire remember?

As I looked at my dad's grave, tremendous emotion grabbed me after all these years. Curtis was meandering down the rows of gravestones as I broke into tears and shouted, "Why did you leave me?" The anger in my tone surprised me because, after all, it wasn't my dad's choice to have a massive heart attack and leave a wife and two young children to fend for themselves. I thought my anger was irrational, but later I realized that, ironically, it came from love and longing.

I missed my Dad all my life, but I didn't truly realize the feeling of abandonment that was lurking below the surface. I never expressed it to my mom, sister, or anyone. While we shared death, we didn't talk about it. I guess my mom and relatives thought it would make me sad to talk about my father even though I thought about him all the time. Today, I wish they had told me more stories and brought him to life, rather than have him be just the man in a picture with wire frame glasses holding me in his arms.

Only once did my sister Betty and I discuss our situation, when she was about 11 years old, 4 years older than me. She said, "You know . . . if something happens to Mom, we will be orphans." That scared the hell out of me. I was too young to realize that she had been thinking about my Dad's death and was probably very anxious, too. Her recollections of him and the night he died were much more vivid. It was after this that I became clingy with my mother to the point my aunts said I was a "Momma's boy." That didn't feel good either, but I needed my mother's reassuring presence. I was afraid and didn't want to lose her.

Although I had wonderful uncles who took me under their collective wings and shared music, golf, fishing, and just hanging out with me, I didn't have a "real" dad. I didn't even know how it felt to have a father: all I knew was that I just felt different. I didn't feel anger: just a sense of absence—-a void.

In second grade, I recollect having to make a tie rack out of the inner cardboard tube from a roll of toilet paper as part of a Father's Day project. I came home and told my mom about it. She diplomatically suggested that I give the tie rack to my Uncle Zig, a bachelor who lived in the flat below us. He was the most present male figure in my early life, and very special. He served in WWII in Italy with the First Mountain Division but never talked of his exploits. We hung out together with his dog, Phony, a short little mongrel that liked to cuddle up with me when I lay on the living room floor. My uncle said he was "a Heinz 57 variety breed," in other words, just a mutt. We loved that dog, and I loved Uncle Zig because he made me feel like I mattered and that I was capable.

He watched out for me and bandaged me up when I fell on my bike and opened a gash on my forearm. He was there when it mattered. But my grandmother used to say, "Zig wasn't the same when he came back from the war." He died at the age of 52 from alcoholism.

I didn't like people feeling sorry for me, even if it was well intentioned. Once I tried out for Little League baseball. I went through the drills, shy and unsure of myself, not talking to the coaches or anyone else for that matter. I didn't know anyone, so I stood off by myself.

I wasn't a stellar player. My baseball experience was playing "wall ball" with Butch, my friend who lived next door, or slow-pitch in the alley where hitting the ball in the yards was an automatic "out." Sometimes I had a game of catch with my cousin, Paul, or with another friend.

Shaking My Fist

I shook my fist at God today
Damning Him for taking your life
Challenging His love and compassion
And trying to understand His thinking.

But God doesn't think,
Not in the ways we do
There's no logic, rhyme, or reason for His actions
They just are, and we have to accept them.

That's His way—that's the way it is
There's no due process and justice
Concerning God's will.
So, we're stuck, powerless, and you're gone.

God's mercy seems alien and
Coming in a form different than we understand.
In the meantime, He lets us play in this wondrous world,
Until chance or fate calls us home.

I shook my fist at God today
What can He do about it? Take retribution?
I've taken His best shot,
There is little He can do to hurt me anymore.

After all, isn't He the great benefactor

Of all things in life?

He gave me the ability to get angry.

So I did.

After the drills, the Little League coaches huddled at the pitcher's mound, as we stood around second base. They were determining who would make the team and I heard one coach say, "the Goens' kid doesn't have a dad. He died. Let's take him." Somehow hearing that struck me wrong and I never went back to the ball field. The coach's instincts were honorable, but I didn't want to be treated as special because my dad was dead. I didn't want to make a ball team because of sympathy.

But now, 32 years after his death, I railed at my father's gravesite for abandoning me. I grasped how profoundly I missed my dad even though, as a kid, I never expressed it. In my older fantasies I wondered what it would be like to have dinner with him, to hear his voice, to find out about his politics, and to learn about his passions and ideas. My aunts said that my personality was similar to his. He was intense and a bit of a tease. According to them, the proverbial apple doesn't fall very far from the tree.

Mist of Memories

Memories float on light air,

Seemingly random messages of times past

Triggered by small conversation

And random observation,

All darting into mind

Without warning.

You sit in the back of my brain

Dancing when ignited

By a small expression in word or glance

Creating a mist of recollection that

Soon evaporates and I realize you are gone

forever.

While in college, and home for a break, I talked to my mom about him—asked questions about what he was like. Up in her closet, packed back on a shelf, was a box of mementos she had saved. She opened it and handed me an old tie clasp and a small penknife of his. She also showed me some old black and white pictures and a professionally printed Zenith Corporation newsletter. Both my mom and dad worked at Zenith where they met.

She told me to look at the April, 1946, brochure and said, "Your father got an award for a suggestion he made to the company." Sure enough, there was a picture of my dad and another fellow receiving a $250 check for their suggestion concerning the Coil Department. He and his colleague submitted an idea to build "a model coil winding machine to wind Strator coils for the JJ contract." He and his partner were featured at a steak dinner with "all the trimmings."

He and his colleague both left Zenith and started their own business to carry through on the building of that machine. Six months later, he died from a massive heart attack when he collapsed at home after work.

Finding this information was such a bonus because it gave me a concrete glimpse of a part of his life and contributions. That brochure sparked a bit of insight into my father as someone with a creative and entrepreneurial spirit. Yet, I still wondered about him as a person and what our relationship would have been like.

Although I was angry with my father for dying, I did not feel any of the same emotions with Betsy's death. I wasn't angry with Betsy. Obviously she didn't have a choice either. My reaction to her death was so very different. I just felt the deepest and darkest grief, in part because her death turned the normal natural order of things upside down. Dying from an amniotic embolism is rare and could not have been anticipated by her doctor. The rarity of the cause of her death seemed to give some a different perspective because it was so extraordinary. For me, however, the cause didn't matter, my daughter just died; the odds just added to the loss.

My greatest nightmare came true. I worry about Curtis, at times, because he is a police officer who regularly faces difficult circumstances, but I never thought Betsy's life would be cut short, especially while giving birth.

I was angry with God. The platitudes of ministers about "God's plan" angered me as I looked at little Claire and her baby brother, stripped of their mother, who would have loved and nurtured them unconditionally. Some God, I thought. Was there really a hidden purpose in her death that only God could know and we had to accept? Betsy was dead and there was a higher purpose and good that would come from it? Did people really believe this? Did that belief console them and bring them peace? I couldn't accept it—that all-loving, compassionate God with mysterious plans for us.

Many people find acceptance in their religion or they turn to religion to smooth over the shock and despair that come with incomprehensible loss. For me, it was different. Religion did not help me find acceptance or peace. Religion places death in the hands of a supernatural higher being—God. Phrases like "God's will," "God needed her," "She is with God now," or "She's in a better place" fell mute against the screeching pain of death and loss of my grandchildren's mother and my daughter. Mystical explanations made me feel as if I were a puppet on a small stage controlled by the master puppeteer who pulled people off the stage at his whim. Damn God!

To this day, religion has not been a source of peace and comfort. In fact, cynicism toward religion has grown and my belief has diminished. Maybe my anger continues. I really don't care about God's mysterious ways. Life seems harsh and difficult, and faith in the fairy-tale world of God's love and the prospect of eternal life just doesn't exist for me. My loss was painful and horrendous. I didn't want to surrender to some higher being who could play with my family's destiny. Betsy's death seemed so wrong and I couldn't accept it as part of a "plan" implemented for some mysterious reason.

Did God really need her? I thought he was all-powerful. What could he need? Everything is supposed to be in his hands. Claire and Luke needed her! They had to live with what might have been and confront anger, fear, and guilt.

Sages say that you are only sad for the things you lost and loved the most. For parents, there is nothing they love more than their children. Even though Betsy and I were estranged for a time, we had a great time together in all phases of life. The memories live and the loss persists.

My father's death had one lasting impact on my priorities as an adult. Because I didn't have a father, I wanted to be the best dad possible to Betsy and Curtis. So despite my all-consuming job, I made special time for my kids. Times with Betsy revolved around ice-skating. She always loved jumping and dancing and twirling. When she saw figure skaters at the rink at the shopping mall, she was hooked. We signed her up for lessons and I drove her 45 minutes, each way, into Milwaukee for them.

The 90-minute round trip three times a week was a blessing. We had concentrated time to talk about school, friends, and daily life; at other times we listened to the radio or sometimes we argued about what to listen to. I exposed her to Aaron Copland and Stan Getz, and she introduced me to Chicago the "band." Yes, my daughter introduced me to Chicago, and I came to appreciate jazz-rock, or at least more complicated popular music. So we compromised about music. I stopped playing Shostakovich and she didn't bring up Depeche Mode.

When she went to Europe for the year in 1990, I gave her Aaron Copland's Appalachian Spring and The Lincoln Portrait. I told her that if she missed home, she should listen to this recording because she will feel America. Her year in Aix-en-Provence was a highlight in her life as she visited eleven European countries while studying French as an exchange student from the University of Wisconsin–Madison.

Sometimes you do the right thing without knowing it. Once, while Betsy was at the university, I was supposed to make a formal presentation to educators in Madison, Wisconsin. Since I was in town, I called her and asked, "How about having lunch?"

She said, "Great, Dad, I need a good hamburger. Let's go to the Nitty Gritty," which was a student hangout off State Street.

Well, it turned out that the organization for which I was presenting, without my prior knowledge, was going to recognize me as the "Wisconsin Educator of the Year." They didn't tell me about this award, so I missed the annual lunch, because I was having a hamburger with Betsy off of State Street.

I got back to the conference and friends were wondering where I had gone. I laughed and told them that I had lunch with my daughter. To this day, I'm grateful for that decision and would make it again; nothing can compare to spending the short time we have in life with the people we love. Awards can wait. That award, while nice, just didn't compare to going to Nitty Gritty with my hamburger-famished daughter.

Betsy and I were alike in many ways: intense and passionate. We were very close and she once told me that she was proud of me. Her sense of justice was bruised by the divorce and that resulted in the paralyzing hiatus in our relationship. In those five years, I lost track of her life—those little inconsequential details about what she did, thought, felt, and experienced. Perspective on her life was lost. The big things, like birthdays or weddings, don't create the closeness of a relationship. It's the small details and events that add vibrancy to the bigger colors of life and provide understanding. When those vanish, relationships atrophy.

The day before Betsy died, I called her about Luke's impending birth. I told her how excited I was about having a grandson and finished the conversation with these last words: "I love you, Betsy." Those words express everything—the deep feeling between father and daughter, but also the depth of loss and pain I experienced from her death. Tolstoy said, "Only people who are capable of loving strongly can also suffer great sorrow; but the same necessity of loving serves to counteract their grief and heals them . . . Grief never kills."

All parents who lose a child understand this at some level: some more, some less, some sooner, some later. But at the time of your loss, it's difficult to know that the love you experienced and the corresponding grief will help heal the tremendous ache in your heart and the pain of a lost future with its promise and spirit. The ability to right any remaining fractures in my relationship with Betsy dissipated with her last breath. I was left with only three things—beautiful memories, a commitment to her children, and a renewed commitment to continue living with purpose and meaning.

We Shall Meet Again

We shall meet again
When worldly things dissolve
And pure love shines forth.

We shall meet again
When our hearts sing
The song of grace and forgiveness.

We shall meet again
When the mist of earthly illusions evaporate
And our inner light is free.

We shall meet again
When our souls arise and we dance together
In the spirit of loving-kindness.

≈ 4 ≈

What We Leave Behind

I don't know what to say or think—It is so strange not being with my family—the people that mean the most to me on this special day. Know that I am there in mind and spirit. And I will be thinking about each and every one of you—I love you all so much—words can't express the intensity. Feel my spirit—it's there! Your daughter and sister and most importantly friend to you all,

—Betsy, Christmas 1990

PS: Eat cookies and bread pudding for me!

Fear stalks the lonely. Everyone who grieves the loss of a loved one feels a deep sense of longing for his or her company. We yearn to keep their memory alive, because over time, we know that memories fade a bit and details get fuzzy. We don't forget the significant dates. Birthdays, graduations, and first job remain soldered in our minds, but the minor details of circumstances can dissolve. In addition, our minds and memory are exclusive to our perspective and to us. What we remember may be different from what others recollect.

In one of Betsy's letters to me while she was in college, she makes a joking reference to a shirt that I wore. To this day, I still cannot remember what shirt it was and why it made such an impression on her. I didn't know I had any amusing shirts—my wardrobe is an inexpensive version of Brooks Brothers and actually quite conservative, with the exception of some old hockey t-shirts. That memory, however, is lost to me. But to her, it was a humorous indication of our connection.

As her grandfather, I worry that Claire, in particular, will forget her mother: those wonderful times she recalled in a conversation I had with her when she was five years old, one year after her mother died. All of these memories become a mosaic of a life: a story or narrative that keeps the person human and alive in our minds—not as abstractions or symbols, but examples of a person's humanity.

Her funeral services underscored that we remember people through stories. In the eulogies, in the reception line afterward, and in the written notes, friends and relatives told stories woven around their association and experiences with Betsy.

Stories are such remarkable and poignant gifts. Stories, not data or metrics, facts or figures, capture our humanity. Too bad our society underrates them. In almost every civilization, stories have played a great role in helping people understand their society, culture, history, and values. Stories about Betsy added depth and texture and helped me understand her life and contributions to others. They far outpace the ability of technology and e-mail to do so. The subtleties of personal emotion and inflection are lost on technology. If the eyes are the windows to the soul, technology is blind and texting is tone deaf.

In these stories I saw Betsy more clearly than ever before. Sure, she was my daughter. I helped raise her. I was connected to her biologically and emotionally. Yet, as her father, I didn't always perceive her clearly and objectively as she traveled down the road of life. My vision was obscured because, as parents, we can never fully see our children objectively at any age. Objectivity is not a perspective parents have. Maybe we all think that our children were raised in Garrison Keillor's Lake Wobegon—they are above average and free of any foibles or imperfections.

The perspective of others gave me a sharper picture of Betsy's life. Stories validated the hopes I had for her as an adult. No one talked of resumes, degrees, jobs, titles, or social standing or prominence. They focused on her inner core: her being and her principles, values, and behavior. All of the things really that parents are most concerned about; they answer the question, what kind of person will my child grow up to be?

One thing is clear. When we die, we leave only one thing behind. Our character! Our character defines the essence of who we were, how we lived, and what we thought was important in life. When all is said and done, people remember our temperament and personality, what we believed, our values, conduct, demeanor, and our behavior. And yes, they recall our foibles and quirkinesses: the verbal and nonverbal expressions we use, our penchant for certain foods, our gait and physical movements, or our weird obsessions.

At the formal ceremonies and in letters and notes, I was reminded constantly of Betsy's character. They talked about her compassion, empathy, fairness, and her "gentle manner." They told stories of the decisions she made, particularly about being a mother and staying home to raise her two children. They highlighted her unique sense of humor and her passion that went back to her strong adherence to the principles of justice, goodness, and fairness. In addition, her personality came to life in small tidbits and comments about her love of people, her exuberance, and her individuality.

Her friend Jamie wrote this:

> Betsy loved my little boy, Mac. What a perfect choice my husband and I made selecting she and Bill as his Godparents. She took the role seriously and faithfully loved and nurtured him, as well as spoiling him. At our house it was always so exciting to receive a package from B.B. as we lovingly referred to her.

One of her good friends in Florida, Tami, wrote a letter to Claire and Luke about their mother. A segment of that letter defines her idiosyncrasies.

> She kept every Chinese fortune in her wallet that she ever got out of a fortune cookie. She was very sentimental and kept most cards that were ever given to her. She loved to listen to jazz on the radio. She loved the musical artists Sting and Seal. She didn't go for the slapstick humor movies, but loved the dramas. McDonalds, loved it; brownies, loved them too (no wonder we were such good friends!)
>
> She also believed that you should never be a cheapskate when it came to your make-up foundation, your haircuts or items that would fill your home. She bought expensive foundation but used

Noxzema (cheap face cleanser) to clean her face. Her skin of course was flawless, like a peach. She was also very organized. Every bin was labeled and put away. If she was leaving the house, she always had a tote bag ready to go with things to entertain and care for Claire. With some help from Claudia, another good friend, she taught herself how to sew and made curtains, pillows and Luke's baby comforter. Of course the stuff always looked like it was designer made.

On any trip that she made you could be assured that she would walk up to a local police officer and ask them for a patch for her brother Curtis, who as you know, was also a police officer. She always came back with a patch or a phone number of the local station where she could get a patch.

Dreams

I dreamt the other day
of seeing you.
You walked toward me,
with an outstretched hand.

Your smile and energy shone and
My heart beat with excitement at seeing you.

Ever since the ninth day of March,
years ago,

I wanted to see you again, and

feel your embrace and smell

your hair and feel the warmth

of your hand in mine.

I reached out, and then the light

of the early morning

hit my eyes and I awoke,

alone

in bed

as the dream and aura

slowly evaporated

in the unfolding of a new day.

What a gift for Claire and Luke! This peek into Betsy's nature provided them with a concrete view and portrayed who she was in human and understandable terms.

What Tami forgot to say was how much Betsy loved Ketchup—she put it on things other people would not even think about. Betsy wrote from France:

> . . . the food service just decided to go on strike. They were going to have fries today too! Adri [her roommate] and I are so typically American—we take a sack with salt, pepper, and Ketchup in it. Do we get stared at by the "Frenchies"—but hey, that makes us happy, so there! Not going to conform, you know! The Ketchup is Heinz by the way. The best!

The stories about her also identified her principles. Jamie wrote:

> How blessed I have been to call her my best friend. She always remembered the little things of importance to me such as the dates of my parents' deaths. I always received a phone call to check on me those days. She listened and lovingly understood and set me straight when necessary. My life is much richer because of her and will never be the same without her.

I hope these stories provide Claire and Luke with a model for their lives. Death can turn people into abstractions. These stories about Betsy erase the abstract so that Claire and Luke can get to see their mother as others did and understand the impact she had because of the way she lived. Stories have the power to help them know their heritage and where they came from.

I was never a very religious person, but Betsy became involved in church and studied the Bible. She searched for positive principles and an understanding of the importance of forgiveness in life. She seemed to have found it in religion. Others may find it in other ways. The important thing is that she treated everyone with respect and dignity and love. She saw the uniqueness of people as a measure of the humanity that connects us all. But Betsy isn't here physically; now she lives only in stories and vignettes.

I am concerned, at times, about whether Betsy's values and character will become a part of Luke's and Claire's lives. Her approach to life and her search for purpose and meaning are invaluable lessons. With Betsy gone, what values and principles guide their upbringing? The power and influence of modeled behavior is of great significance.

I want my grandchildren to be raised in a nurturing aura of "goodness" where respect, dignity, decency, honesty, integrity, and compassion are evident in all relationships and interactions.

As mentioned earlier, I feared losing access to and contact with my daughter's children. Being cut out of the picture with my grandkids was a frightening possibility. I was besieged by the tangle of emotions. My son-in-law, Bill, allayed those fears. He committed to ensuring that Mary, Curtis, and I have contact with the kids and are active parts of their lives. I could not ask for more.

Bill remarried about 21 months after Betsy died and expanded his family with a stepson. His new "blended" family changed the context for him and for my grandchildren. Many of these families fail because of the conflict of values, territorial behavior, ego, and defensive behavior.

Sometimes I worry about the strain on his new wife, Heather, living in the context of Betsy's death. I know it isn't easy, particularly because of the publicity surrounding a rare maternal death. Right away, Heather was in a tough spot. She was in a new marriage and family because of a tragic death that garnered some newspaper publicity and because of Bill's job as a golf professional with many business and social contacts. In addition, her son, six at the time, became a member of a new family, complete with a younger sister and a baby.

Making this type of new family work would not be easy under normal circumstances, but in this case, it was made more difficult because grief was a veil my family and I wore. Betsy's death . . . Bill's dating . . . a new marriage! This was quite a ride at a speed that, for me, at least initially, was difficult to adjust to. I was struggling just to live with the specter of Betsy's death and the changes it brought. Facing a new family structure so soon was a huge challenge for me. The death of my daughter and its impact with the overwhelming grief does not dissipate easily or, in fact, ever. It is hard not to think back to what was.

Where would I fit in? I was no longer a direct member of the family, and felt like I was a carry-over from a former life. The kids had three grandfathers and grandmothers, plus an unknown number of relatives from Heather's and Bill's families.

At times I felt like an appendage and a living memory of a saddening, tragic event. In these circumstances, I'm not sure people know where to put the family of a dead mother or father in a new blended family. Claire and Luke see me as their grandfather, and Claire certainly remembers who her mother is. For Luke, he sees me as a grandfather and the father of Uncle Curtis and his "first mother," Betsy.

Yet, just below the surface of my sorrow and fears, I felt compassion for Heather and hoped that the kids would be loved and that Bill would be happy. Yet, I realized that with Betsy gone the whole dynamic was different. I worried about Claire, and I felt a sinking feeling knowing that Luke would never know his mother.

I am sure Heather was also overwhelmed by the complexity of the situation and the intricacy of the relationship—her "former" family, her new relations, Bill's family, and Betsy's family: pretty complex with many different angles and needs.

To say there were not tensions as a result of this new situation would be a lie. There were. Under normal circumstances combining families in a new structure would be a challenge in and of itself. For me, seeing someone else in the "mothering" role instead of Betsy was painful and a tangible reminder of Betsy's absence. She's not here! What would be different if she were? God, I wish the kids could have her back! She loved being a mother and Claire needed her! I needed her! But as Robert DeNiro said in the movie *Heat*, "It is what it is! It is what it is!"

One day, while Heather and I were alone in the home surrounded by all the furnishings and décor that was there when Betsy was alive, I said, "Can we talk?" She looked at me warily.

"I want you to know, that I understand it's difficult for you with a new family. It isn't easy," I said, as she leaned back in the leather couch and crossed her legs. "I just want the best for the kids—just love them and take care of them."

She looked at me and I could see her eyes moistening. The moment had a slight tension to it. She was quiet. "I know Betsy wasn't perfect and when someone dies like she did, they can become bigger than life. People may put them on a pedestal."

She listened and said, "It has been difficult. I keep hearing from people about how perfect she was . . . her sewing, her relationships! I'm a different person!"

"Just be who you are, Heather. No one wants you to be Betsy. Just be yourself. All I want is for the kids to be loved and to be happy."

I hesitated, and said, "I have fears too. I am afraid sometimes that I will lose my connection to Claire and Luke. I'm in a strange position, too. My fear is that as you and Bill make a family, I could be locked out—I am no longer a father in this new relationship. I'm a carryover from the past."

Heather looked shocked and then said, "Oh. I would never do that. I have a very close relationship with my dad and grandfather. I would never do that." Tears welled up in her eyes. "If something happened to me, I would want my father to be a part of my son's life. I would not want my former husband to cut them out."

Suddenly, I felt safer. Only a face-to-face discussion could help both of us. E-mails or other technological advances could never bring the two people in our situation together. We hugged tightly and pressure subsided and I could feel a deeper connection to the woman who took my daughter's position in the family.

Betsy wasn't faultless, but she was my daughter and the mother of Claire and Luke. Loving the kids should supersede adult issues or egocentric needs. Claire, in particular, needed understanding and compassion because Betsy's death was a gargantuan blow to her as it would be to any child. Sometimes we forget the extent to which children grieve, too. To many people, death is abstract, without texture or power on adults and children.

Time has helped me realize that people who love and care for the children of others are a wonder. For that, there is a special station in life, and we should be grateful.

"I am sorry for your loss." I heard that clichéd expression time and time again, but the perspective is wrong: it's not singular. In reality, death brings multiple losses—some of which are evident, and others unveil themselves over time.

Through all of this, a friend wondered how I was "doing." What a curious word. *Doing* usually concerns some sort of activity. Doing something—acting, planning, behaving. With grieving, it is more a state of mind and a condition of the heart, rather than simply doing. You can't *do* grief out of your system like when you take an antibiotic to oust an infection or to relieve pain.

I replied, "Doing? I don't know."

"It must be difficult facing such a loss," my friend said.

"Loss?" I said, in an almost antagonistic way, but I caught myself and said, "Not loss. Losses. Losses! When Betsy died, I lost a lot of things. Not only is she gone and I lost my daughter, but it also changed my relationship with relatives and friends, and I don't have the kind of influence I would've had helping Betsy raise the kids. I lost the ability to create more memories with her: to share her company . . . to have her understanding and love. She's not here!"

"But you made a commitment to see them frequently," he mentioned, seeing my passion rise.

"Yeah, Bill has been great about it. But with Betsy out of the picture, I lost a level of candor I had when she was alive. I walk on eggshells a bit now. Besides, I lost the phone calls from her asking for so-called fatherly advice."

With her death, I also lost a future. The chance to be a part of her everyday life with all of its trials and tribulations is gone, and the direct father-daughter relationship died with her. I could no longer share time with her, and the hole in my life cannot be filled by anyone else. The weight of these losses buckled my knees then and is present today every time I see the news, read a newspaper, or see movies where the death of son or daughter is reported. To this very day, the emotion and pain returns and my heart aches for those devastated by the death of a child of any age.

In so-called "magical" moments, I wonder how my relationship with my daughter would have developed and how my role as a grandparent would be different if she was alive. I lost the ability to share my life experiences and wisdom with her as she moved through her life's journey.

In this conversation with my friend, I was certain to mention how much I value Bill's understanding and compassion toward Betsy's mother and me. But the dynamics are different, and sometimes I sense pressure on him in his new family structure. But the past cannot be forgotten because it would be a disservice to the children. Betsy's death is the biggest event in their lives up to this point, next to their births, that is, and it will have a lasting, life-long impact.

The kids are doing well, but the traditions of our family are lost because the players are different. The possibilities for the kids are different. The family interests are different. We were a skating family, and I'm sure that Betsy would have taught both kids to ice skate. That's okay, as long as they get involved in positive activities that they like and enjoy. It's the values that matter. Luke is involved in roller hockey and enjoys playing outdoors in Florida's 80-degree heat.

Betsy's impact and influence on me is confined to what it was, not what it can be in the future. As parents, we learn from our children, too, as they do from us. Just as I discovered her impact on others, I also learned things about myself from her life and example.

Learning is not just a one-way proposition—moving from parent to child. As I age, I often wonder what relationship Betsy and I would have forged. I am sure the warmth of her affection and concern will be sorely missed . . . yet another of my losses.

Through the tragic circumstance of death, we become less cavalier about life and mortality. We learn about heartbreak. Grief and loss. Losses—multiple losses.

The Fog

It's been almost two years since the
fog of loss filtered into my life,
slowly but completely, after
you left us. Time seems
opaque and useless to measure
the depth of distance from
that fateful day in March.

Fog changes things—surrounds
us in suffocating closeness,
searing into our bones, causing
uncertainty, outpacing
the reach of logic, altering
perspective, and awakening
the rabid dog of fear.

Images become silhouettes,
then vague reflections, and
circles into smoky haze
of illusions and thoughts
connected by the garland of fear.

The self-enclosed capsule
of fog separates us from our

comrades journeying through grief
and insulates us from the logic
and the pleas of those who care for us.

Grief has a haze all its own and
reflects the wings of memories past
and in a paradoxical way, clarifies
the life we live today.
In a way, the fog, once lifted,
gives us the gift of new eyes and the
realization that what's tangible
is ephemeral and what we can't grasp
is the substance we need

$$\approx 5 \approx$$

Obligation

"You know, Grandpa, you called me Betsy six times today,"
Claire said, looking at me with a wide grin.

When Do You Know?

When do you know it's the last time?

We walk through life thinking we'll be back,

that we will come again,

looking forward to returning to the familiar.

Some day—one day—

it will be the last time.

But we don't know when

it's the last sunset,

the last kiss, or

the last time we say,

I love you.

"I know, Betsy, . . . I mean Claire," I said with a laugh. "It's just that sometimes you remind me so much of your mom. You even jump around like she did when she was your age."

"Tell me a story about when you were a little boy," she replied. She loved family anecdotes and took special delight in childhood tales about Betsy and Curtis. She liked hearing about them as kids, our vacations, and small, insignificant family routines. She especially liked the story about Slapshot, our cat, laying in wait under the dining room table to ambush Curtis and jump at his skinny "chicken legs" when he walked around in his shorts.

She concentrates and soaks up all the details of the events, and laughs at the exploits of her mom and uncle when they were small. Claire is almost like a living memory, certainly an instant recollection, of my times past with Betsy. At times, it feels like I live in a parallel reality reliving flashes of times past but this time with my grandchildren.

Betsy lives within Claire and shows herself in quick, unexpected, innocent movements. The way she sits, her hand motions, her expressiveness and her dancing and twirling are almost exact replicas of her mother when she was Claire's age. Even the way she moves her mouth when she smiles and her sense of humor merge the past with the present.

All of these small incidences are wonderful, soulful reminders of life. In a great sense, I am lucky because it's as if Betsy isn't too far away. I catch a glimpse of her presence in a snippet of movement or expression. Claire brings to life remnants from another time. Reminders that Betsy may not be as far away as I think. Our connection is now reflected in the natural and innocent behavior and instincts of her daughter.

I cannot leave Luke out of the picture. He carries a bit of Betsy in him, too. When he visited the farm where I live, I saw him running down the hill, and in a brief instant, he took me back in time to Wisconsin at the Kettle Moraine State Forest when Betsy and Curtis emerged from the woods and ran through a sea of grass. Luke fell forward, down the hill, and then picked himself up, ran over to me, and said, "Grandpa, I run faster than my body." I couldn't stop laughing.

DNA must be powerful because he runs just like Betsy did with his legs flailing outward with every stride. I guess that foretells the fact that he will never be a world-class track star. Luke's expressiveness and affectionate hugs are also in harmony with Betsy when she was his age. All of these moments are true gifts.

The reality, however, is that even though I have the gift of short reincarnations of her life and existence through my grandchildren, Betsy is dead. The soft breeze of those moments always warms my heart, yet the void created by Betsy's death, cannot be replaced, even by the endearing love of grandchildren.

The meandering road from grief to peace and acceptance, is difficult. Painful demons inhabit the cold darkness of death's loneliness, obscuring and disorienting the purpose of daily life. The path is hard and tenuous, I've found, and it cannot be traversed at turbocharged speed. It has its own pace and rhythm. Everyone must travel it at his or her own tempo, in his or her own way, and with his or her own rituals.

Acceptance that life changed and will never be the same for me was crushing to admit. It felt like I was giving up a critical portion of my past and of life itself. Maybe that drove me back to the typical religious rituals of my earlier life. They certainly couldn't hurt, but could they help?

Even before Betsy's death, religion had faded from importance in my life, although occasionally I slipped back into candle lighting and saying a prayer. I like the familiar smell of candles in church and lighting them is more of a personal tribute and expression of hope than religious conviction.

Montreal is a city that has always had positive energy for me. I would go there by myself when I first came out East in the early '90s. Many times I drove my black, streamlined motorcycle there and buzzed around the city. Mourning the loss of my job, my divorce, and my estrangement from Betsy, I felt desperate and gravitated to the churches in the "old" city. One church, in particular, Chapelle des Marins [Sailors Church], is the oldest wooden church in North America and has a simple seafarer's theme. The other church is the lavish Notre Dame Cathedral, complete with architecture, stained-glass windows, and the extravagant flourish of hierarchical formality.

I preferred the small, modest wooden church. When I was feeling low, I would go there and light candles for my mom, father, uncles, and aunts, all of whom died years ago. My old life as a kid, going to Catechism must have kicked in. I would light a special candle for Betsy so some day she would talk to me again and get through the cloud of divorce. Maybe the candles worked—because eventually she did. At the time, I was covering my bets. A sad reason to cling to a remnant of religion that I never really fully embraced or understood. I am not a true believer. Something happened long before Betsy died that caused me to drift away from organized religion. Even the crises in my life did not bring me back.

After Betsy's death, I made a pilgrimage back to the old wooden church and lit candles again—this time for her and my grandchildren. I even prayed that Betsy would look after them and hoped that the symbolic light of the candle would provide guidance for Claire and Luke. Lighting a candle is a hopeful act, albeit for a fee in church. I was sending positive energy into the world. My attitude toward rituals changed a bit. God was not really the "source" or a part of the equation anymore. To me, the candle sent out the energy of hope and love.

At times I harkened back to an earlier era when I went to the big Catholic Church at the corner of our neighborhood. As a child, religion and death were a mystery. An all-powerful God would punish me if I died in sin—for taking the Lord's name in vain, or for violating the Sabbath, or for eating meat on Friday. As a child, the concepts of hell and purgatory were frightening. I could never figure out this "limbo" thing. Who thought of these ideas? How could God be loving and so punishing and petty? Who could meet those standards? I was doomed, I thought. But in a curious way, all of this was liberating. Would God really make up these silly concepts that seemed filled with superstitious hokum? After all, the religious texts were written hundreds of years ago in a male-dominated, hierarchical society. The people who lived then had no concept of the earth as being round, awareness of people on the other side of the planet, or the equality of people, particularly women. They were married to superstition.

The devastation of death, however, pushed me to this sanctuary called church, but while sitting there, my thoughts did not turn to God. The Bible did not provide comfort. Maybe my heart was hardened by the starkness of death. Maybe I never did buy into the concept of a higher being and the fairy-tale stories of virgin births, walking on water, resurrections, loaves and fishes, and water and wine. To me, God's plan was of no concern. My daughter had died! Nothing was going to change that. There was not going to be any miraculous ending. I didn't believe in miracles. God was irrelevant to me.

What did help me on this journey through despair was poetry. The fluid voice of poets and their passages through life with its joys and travails connected me to a humanity greater than myself. In poems of people I did not even know, I found a bond that helped me through loneliness into a quiet, almost peaceful solitude. Poems about the simple aspects of life and the deep emotions of love and joy and death and sorrow smoothed the pathway to acceptance of what was.

I didn't feel isolated in my anguish, and I felt a part of an invisible community that provided me with a modicum of solace and tranquility. I wasn't alone! I was connected through poignant stories and experiences of other human beings facing difficult and heartbreaking circumstances.

Poetry, with its poignancy and rhythms, currents and phrases, levels and depths—its mysteriousness and humanity spoke to me more than religious writings. The human spirit spoke from the stanzas and provided perspective and hope.

Music was also a sanctuary, even, ironically, some religious hymns. For some reason, old American hymns spoke to me more than Bible passages, gospels, psalms, or church services. One American hymn, arranged by Aaron

Copland, "Shall We Gather at the River" resonated a hopeful message, particularly this stanza:

Soon we'll reach the silver river,
Soon our pilgrimage will cease;
Soon our happy hearts will quiver
With the melody of peace

"Simple Gifts" always joined Betsy and me together, a piece of music we both enjoyed and shared. Every time I listen to it, I somehow feel closer to her. In a curious way, I feel that the chords and force of emotion in that piece connects us. The old Shaker hymn, written in 1848 by Joseph Brackett, has a simple yet noble and profound message.

'Tis the gift to be simple, 'tis the gift to be free
'Tis the gift to come down where we ought to be,
And when we find ourselves in the place just right,
'Twill be in the valley of love and delight.
When true simplicity is gain'd,
To bow and to bend we shan't be asham'd,
To turn, turn will be our delight,
Till by turning, turning we come 'round right

I gave a tape of it to her when she went to Europe, she played it at her wedding, we played it at her funeral, and I played it when I remarried. To me, that piece is emblematic of her life. As a mother, she came down where she was supposed to be.

I get emotional when I hear "Simple Gifts." Music has a unique facility, like the sense of smell, to arouse feelings, memories, and the aura of presence. The memories rise to the surface like waves that originate in the deep sea of emotion and sorrow. They make me pause and feel the moment. Music truly nourishes the soul and resurrects heartfelt feelings and emotions.

Her death tore the very fabric of my life just like ripping a gaping hole in a spider's web. Like the spider, I had to recognize and accept that my life changed and had to weave a new wholeness out of what remained. The new woven pattern, while reminiscent of the old, was not the same; it has different strands and patterns. The relationships of the past must be melded with a new unfolding reality.

Unexpected losses drive home the true value of relationships. We hold on to small things as we learn to live in the vacuum of loss. I still have a necktie Betsy bought for me in France, two pictures she purchased in Prague, a coffee mug she gave me for when I was on the road, a potpourri of family pictures, and a small Christmas ornament that I have hanging from the latch of my window. I keep it there throughout the whole year. All are visible reminders of her presence.

Creating this new wholeness is a road that helped lead me beyond the dark journey of despair. To me, this meant revitalizing an openness to life and creating a sense of belonging to myself, to the world around me and to the relationships I have that are necessary for my sense of efficacy. Relationships form our reality, and my relationship to Betsy, while so very prominent and lasting, is not of this life now. Death did not sever that relationship, it just has a different but intense and deeply emotional form now.

As I struggled with this new reality, well-meaning friends asked if I was able to "move on." I hated that term. Move on? *Move on?* My daughter died for Chrissakes! I didn't just have an argument or lose a job—my daughter died! You just don't walk away or leave your feelings and seek diversion and live your old life.

The term *move on* sounds trivial and not really appropriate because it lacks responsibility and certainly is absent of obligation. I could make a mess of things and just move on—leave. Moving on doesn't require coming to terms with reality or with my responsibility and obligations to what remains of my family and myself. In a sense, it connotes, to me, running away from rather than facing circumstances and life as it is and coming to terms with it.

The term *moving ahead* speaks more to understanding and healing the paralyzing depths of anguish. By accepting reality, I thought I could achieve some sense of purpose and acceptance of life as it is and move ahead with living—but not forget. I felt I had choices. I could run away and move on and live a self-deceptive charade, or I could get stuck on the road of grief and live with what might have been. Both were unacceptable.

Choosing to accept that we own our lives and seeing the beauty of what is possible, even though a devastating loss has altered things forever, is the beginning of progress. We honor all life when we live our own lives with purpose and meaning. There is no going back, and the amnesia of moving on is not realistic or responsible. Moving ahead requires healing that moving on doesn't.

Philosophically it comes down to one thing: to honor Betsy's life I had to live my life to the fullest because she couldn't. Her life was cut short. Why? I will never know nor be able to fully comprehend. She lived her life with such energy and passion that I could not squander the remaining years I have by failing to contribute the best I can. She always had the commitment and verve to live life totally and to do what is right. I have to carry on that spirit.

The choice to move ahead did not mean forgetting Betsy. Far from it. In fact choosing to contribute, be creative, and do what I can with my life is the best way to remember and honor who she was. She had dreams that she'll never be able to fulfill. If I wasted my life and dreams I would be dishonoring the life she could not fulfill. I had to commit and engage, because her children need support to find their passion, live with zest, and risk adventure. Just like their mother did.

Life isn't easy but we are alive. While our heart breaks we must use the love that pours from it and see the beauty of what is possible, by connecting with others with compassion, empathy, and love. Grace—acceptance of others with forgiveness and goodwill—is a byproduct of the intense devastation we feel when someone we deeply love dies. Moving ahead comes with the duty to live life with grace and use it for some greater good.

The cocoon of anger and despair wastes the love and understanding that we can bring to life. Tragedies rip the bark off of pretense, materialism, and superficial and trivial endeavors. The painful vulnerability that death brings reminds us of the gift of life that we should cherish and fulfill.

Maybe Einstein was right when he said "True religion is real living; living with all one's soul, with all one's goodness and righteousness," and "Only a life lived for others is a life worthwhile." That's a religion I can buy into.

Betsy's death caused me to recommit to living a life of principle—to respond to others with kindness and love—to make the most of the time I have left on earth. Wisdom can come from life's sadness if we are open to coming to terms with it. A "Native Blessing" from Nancy Wood's book *Spirit Walker*, addresses this well:

Native Blessing

Bless these circumstances.

Bless the hardship and the pain.

Bless the hunger and the thirst.

Bless the locusts and the drought.

Bless the things that do not turn out right.

Bless those who take all and give not.

In these circumstances, find growth.

In growth, find clarity.

In clarity, an inner vision.

$\Longleftarrow$ 6 $\Longrightarrow$

Letters

Write and tell all—I love the letters—read them over and over!
—Betsy, France, 1991

Betsy was a prolific note and letter writer. She learned that from her mother who mastered the disciplined art of letter writing. So it was a trait handed down from generation to generation. Betsy's Grandmother Meyer wrote weekly letters to her four children. She always started her letters with a sentence about the weather and temperature and then would go on to describe the doings and events of what she was up to. I used to ask my wife with an affectionate tease, "What's happening in the exciting metropolis of Black River Falls?"

I found some delight in these letters that described small town America with detailed descriptions of church activities and the sagas of aunts, uncles, nieces, and nephews. Joy characterized her stories and the interactions of her everyday life. In fact, if we didn't receive one, I wondered what was going on; a testament to the value of these handwritten, margin-to-margin two-sided letters.

Betsy followed that tradition and took to writing notes and letters, whether she was in college at the University of Wisconsin or studying in France. We always taught our kids to say "thank you," and that a written expression was particularly special. Notes have an impact much greater than most other forms of written communication. A friend wrote to me after Betsy's death: "One of the many things she did to make me feel special was to send me notes and cards, all of which I still have."

I tried to follow suit as well. When I was superintendent of schools, I made it a point to communicate personally with staff, parents, and the community. My last school district had over 1000 employees, 7500 children, and about 60,000 citizens. Obviously I couldn't communicate personally with everyone every day, but when a personal expression was appropriate, I either met with the individual face to face or wrote a personal letter or note.

I asked my executive secretary for a list of all employees in the district with their birthdays. She asked, "You want the name of every employee and their birth date? What are you to do with those?" I replied, "I want to send them each a personal birthday note."

"That's great. I'll order some birthday cards today."

"No, that's not necessary. I just want to write a personal note, not send a card. Just order some blank, plain stationary cards."

"But there are a thousand people employed in the district. Isn't it easier just to send them a birthday card and sign it?"

"Yes, but it's not personal. Everybody's birthday is a special day, and a commercial card just doesn't hack it. Kathy, I just need the list of birthdays each week so that I can write these notes. Because we are a large organization doesn't mean we can't be personal."

People deserve genuine communication. By acknowledging our employees in an individual way, I wanted to model for them how to work with children, colleagues, parents, and community members. Doing business shouldn't be reduced to techno-communication, analytics, or jargonized mishmash.

The importance of letters was brought home to me in an even more potent way. In 2004, I completed my book manuscript, *Soft Leadership for Hard Times*. I thought I was finally finished with the manuscript when the editor called and said that I had to check a reference because he was not sure it was correct. Irritating as it was to have to dig up an obscure citation, I reluctantly headed to the basement and started rummaging through boxes to find the research paper and reference.

I remember the date: September 23rd, just six months after Betsy died and two days before my birthday.

In my rummaging, I found a storage box that had been sealed for years. My curiosity got the best of me and I opened it and had begun leafing through the materials and books when I came upon a black Allen Edmonds shoebox. Who could resist a mysterious black shoebox that was taped shut?

So I opened it and found a few old newspaper clippings, notes from friends, long forgotten mementos, and old business cards of mine. Then in the middle of the box, I discovered two card-sized envelopes and a ragged partially torn envelope with a letter in it.

With my curiosity growing, I opened the two card envelopes. To my utter shock and astonishment, I found a couple of birthday cards from Betsy that she had sent to me 11 years earlier. Two days before my birthday, and I received birthday cards from my deceased daughter, seemingly coming out of the cosmos and initiated by an inopportune phone call requiring me to complete a laborious task! Synchronicity, I thought. As I sat alone in the dim light of the basement, my heart started racing. I broke down in tears at this unexpected and precious gift from beyond the rational universe.

I sat for a few stunned minutes and then opened the tattered envelope and found another surprise—a birthday letter written in 1988 by Betsy on quaint University of Wisconsin "Bucky Badger" stationery.

The letter, written in pencil, was a treasure—a true miracle. When I first received it over a decade prior to that day, I never thought it would be the most valuable letter of my life. I don't really remember saving those cards and the letter, but I'm glad I did. Friends have accused me of being a bit of a pack rat who is emotionally attached to things like old hockey t-shirts and a hodgepodge of dehydrated fountain pens.

Every day, I wished I could magically speak to my daughter just one more time. I even scoured an old answering machine tape to see if I could find a remnant of her voice.

The astounding thing about that letter was that for the first time since March 8th, the day before she died, I could hear her voice and sense her presence through her unique, slanted, left-handed script, complete with cross outs and the little tidbits she wrote vertically in the margins. Betsy's vibrant spirit came alive in her handwriting—her distinctive expressions and her buoyant attitude toward life itself.

The gift of her fundamental nature and spirit in that letter was that it was a true reflection of her soul—the best gift I have ever received on my birthday—or ever will. What a wonderful testament for one human being to leave for another. With time, her letters have become more and more valuable, tangible evidence that love remains through the vibrancy of the written word.

I clutched that letter to my chest and smelled the paper, trying to get a whiff of her essence. But the years of storage and the musty passage of time erased any trace of her scent.

Handwritten letters, especially composed with an old-fashioned fountain pen, speak with an emotional force through their unique script that provides a peek into a person's character and soul. Putting pen to paper is truly a remarkable act because it communicates more than just words.

With time, the letters have become more and more valuable, hard evidence that when someone is gone, love remains. A year before her death, Betsy sent a birthday card to Mary, a genuine and heart-warming gift. If time on the planet was soon to end, a note like this is what we should write to people we love.

Dear Mom,

Happy birthday!!
I love you very much. You're my dearest friend. I appreciate so much the love and support you have always given me. I treasure the times we are able to spend together. Thank you for loving my daughter so much—that is the best gift you have ever given me.
I love you,

Betsy

—*Birthday card: August 2003*

Technology is so inadequate in capturing the essence of a person. Finding a digitized e-mail or a Microsoft Word "document" could never match that handwritten letter with Bucky Badger staring at me from the middle of the stationery. Although we contact people through technology, we certainly do not connect in a soulful, personal, and earnest way. Too much is lost in the antiseptic digitization of our feelings. Facebook cheapens communication and is a vacant way to "connect" with people. It prostitutes the word *friend*. In the end, it's just a hollow phenomenon that delivers less than it purports.

The letter and cards from Betsy reminded me that spending some of our precious minutes in life writing a personal note or letter is a true act of affection that transcends death. They are true and personal expressions of our humanness and love for others.

As a consequence of her letter, I wrote a series of letters to my grandchildren about life, purpose, and meaning. These letters, some of them a bit abstract, may not have been age-appropriate for a five-year-old and a baby, but I hope they will be meaningful in later years, particularly after I'm gone.

The first letter was about letters themselves and was a lesson that was reinforced by their mother and that special day—September 23, 2004. I hope Claire and Luke will continue the tradition of personally writing notes and letters that their mother practiced and that others found so valuable and loving.

Dear Claire and Luke,

Today, fewer people seem to write real letters. Technology has curtailed putting pen to paper. It's a shame, really, because writing letters is an act of love. Letters help us see into a person's character and get a taste of their spirit.

Because I love you both, I want to share with you who I am as a person and what I learned in life. You know me as your Grandpa, but I also want you to know me as a person, what I stand for, and what I tried to teach your mom and Uncle Curtis. Because I live over 900 miles away from you, I thought these letters would do the trick! Grandpa likes to write, and there is nothing more special than writing personal letters.

When you both were very young, each of you enjoyed getting mail. You waited with anxious anticipation for the mail to come when you knew I was sending you a card, letter, or little surprise. I love getting your cards, drawings, and letters, too. I am a pack rat and I save them all, safely tucked away in a shoebox.

Letters are one of the really good and special things in life, particularly when they are from relatives, friends, or neighbors. Handwritten letters are especially nice because they are personal, not like those generic word-processed pieces of business correspondence. Handwritten letters come from the person's heart and provide a small window into who they are as fellow human beings. That's why they are so precious, and why they do more than communicate information.

I love fountain pens for that very reason. Today, few people use them, but they are a wonderful way to write letters and notes. The feel of the pen, the width of the nib, and the smooth flow of the ink make a mystical connection to the physical and spiritual being inside of all of us. We communicate a part of ourselves—more than simply words—when we write with a fountain pen.

Many people your age never have had the experience of writing a letter with a fountain pen. Try it! It will get you in touch with that quiet part of your soul that can only be reached when writing in thoughtful silence and solitude. Your feelings and meaning become clear and time fades into insignificance. Only then can you can find your own true voice as a person and communicate ideas, as well as feelings.

For centuries people have written letters in their own hand. This tradition of letters opens our eyes to times past and gives us a glimpse into the people behind the names and titles. Those letters provide insight, not only into their thoughts, but also into matters of the heart and spirit—their loves, their relationship with God, their understanding of themselves, their values and principles, their wishes and desires, their fears and hopes, and their light and dark sides. These letters connect us to the past and to each other because they highlight our common humanity and journey across time. Those old letters help us gain wisdom and understand ourselves better, too.

Letters live across the ages. They have had a profound impact on history. Martin Luther King's letter from the jail in Birmingham focused the nation on civil rights and led the cry for justice. It sparked a movement that spread across the land. Lincoln's letters to mothers of soldiers killed in action during the Civil War recognized the depth of personal sacrifice the families suffered and the compassion of a president and nation. Your mom's letters when she was in college in France show her zest and love for life.

On a smaller and more personal scale, letters commit us morally and legally. A signed letter carries more than words. We commit our love to others and we pledge our honor through letters. The person's integrity is part of their signature and binds them to their words in a sacred covenant. If that obligation is broken, the person's integrity is questioned and trust dissolves.

Thoughtful, carefully crafted letters have great rewards for the reader! Letters touch our hearts because they are personal, written with pen to paper, each letter of every word shaped by our own hand with its unique script, and crafted word-by-word and sentence-by-sentence. Letter writing is a deep act of love because you are reaching out and sharing with others a portion of the time you have on earth. Each minute and day in life, you know, is precious, and spending a part of it writing a personal letter is a loving act.

After your mother died when you were very young, I found a letter from her that I had saved in a shoebox. She wrote the letter when she was nineteen years old and in college. I discovered it six months after her death when I was sad and filled with the grief of missing her. Finding her letter was a Godsend—it was two days before my birthday. For the first time since she died, I could hear her voice as I read her words, I could see her face and feel her personality in her handwriting, and I could hold something tangible to my heart that came from her heart. I cherish that letter with its vibrant optimism and hope, and I value that tangible expression of her love for me from her own hand. I will pass these letters on to you some day so you, too, can have them and get a sense her unique being.

Letters truly mark that we were here on earth, in this place and time, and that we cared for each other. They are visual reminders of our love and passions. Sometimes, you can even get a sense of the person's presence through a hint of their perfume or after-shave radiating from the paper. Computers and technology can't do that—they flatten communication and make it mono-dimensional, technical, and antiseptic.

One suggestion as you write letters—don't worry about cross-outs. Letters weren't meant to be perfect. Letters are like the electrocardiograms of the soul, marking our being from moment to moment as we write. They show our human vulnerabilities, and they illustrate our thought patterns and reveal the inner workings of our minds and hearts. The spontaneous expressions, sentences, and changes add flare and delight to the letters. There is a wonderful bit of improvisation in letters that is missing from word processed, spell checked, perfectly margin-justified letters from a laser printer.

Your generation has been raised with all kinds of technology—much of it designed to communicate quickly. Today, it seems speed is everything. Technology may be fast and efficient, but it lacks heart and soul. E-mail just doesn't cut it except to exchange a few words about time, place, date, location, and purpose of meetings—simple information, not complex ideas or certainly not expressions from the heart. Technology is a vacuous way to express deep emotion, compassion, or spirit. Pressing keys or talking into a machine lacks the connection hand-written letters have linking paper, pen, hand, mind, heart, and soul. Love and feeling flow through the softness of a pen on paper; they are not found in the staccato hammering of a keyboard.

By now you are probably wondering why all this focus on letters. It is very simple. I live quite a distance from Florida in Connecticut and cannot share my life with you each day. I don't have the opportunity, as much as I would like—to have those spontaneous times when we could talk about life—mine and yours—and learn together about the great events of our times and the large and small issues we all confront every day. I have learned many things in my life, and I would like to share them with you to help you with the things you confront.

In life we experience uplifting, wonderful times, and we also taste the bitter sting of loss and pain. Inexplicable things happen and logic sometimes fails. As time goes by, you will experience all of that, too. I wish I could shield you from the pain of life, but that would be unfair to you because there are great lessons in sad as well as joyful times.

Through life's travails and victories we experience what it means to be human and we can gain the wisdom to celebrate matters of the heart, soul, and spirit. We learn in many different ways. Sometimes, life's events are beyond the mind's capacity to understand fully; they require a heart filled with hope and serenity. Letters tie our whole being together as we express our thoughts, feelings, and dreams.

So, Claire and Luke, I am going to send you letters and share what I learned, as well as spout a little philosophy, too. My friends will tell you that I love debate and I like to philosophize about politics, world affairs, and a host of other things. Ideas and principles are important to me—stimulating and motivating! Philosophy is important, too . . . from the well of principle comes wisdom.

Through these letters, I want you to understand the profound love I have for you both, even though I cannot be with you every day. I also want to touch you in a different way by exposing and sharing myself so you will know me as a real, live, breathing human being. My father died when I was four years old, and I wish to this day that I knew better who he was as a person—his strengths and faults, his foibles and personality, and his thoughts and feelings. I missed him so much and thought of him every day, always wondering how my life would be different if he were there.

Sometimes in life, we get lost for a moment or two. I'm not proud of some of my choices. I've made mistakes and I tried to own up to them and accept the consequences. I'm glad I did because by doing so I learned and, by taking responsibility for my mistakes, I maintained my integrity by paying the consequences and making amends the best I could.

Finally, as you grow old you will see remarkable transformations. Your great-grandmother Goens was born in 1911 and she lived to see the birth of the automobile and saw a man land on the moon. She experienced the advent of the telephone, television, and computers. Your experience will be similar, as is mine. The changes that I have seen are almost overwhelming. Science and technology will inevitably revolutionize your life, too.

Celebrate the wonder of it all. Learn and accept that in life unforeseen things happen. Believe in synchronicity—there are no accidents in life. You are meant to be where you are. Remember you have choices and free will, but also let things emerge— don't press all the time. Not everything that is important can be measured. Practice patience (I'm still working on this!). Enjoy the ride of life. And, don't forget to write letters!

Until next time—I love you!

Grandpa

PS: Letters also have one other thing that other forms of communication lack—a signature. A person's signature is one of a kind, totally unique to that individual, giving us a hint about the person and his or her personality. Sometimes signatures are small, tight, and closed. Other times they are looping, large, and bombastic. In our signatures, we communicate more than our names—they often signal our approach to life itself and our personality. What a beautiful way to end a letter. So, here's Grandpa's signature!

≈ 7 ≈

Relationships

Dad, how awesome to have talked to you last night. I was just standing there—like I was waiting for a call from my Dad. It's funny too 'cause Adri and I were talking about our relationship no more than a half-hour before. I was so happy I couldn't sleep!

—Betsy in Aix-en-Provence

According to scientists, all there is to reality is relationships. Betsy's death shattered a part of my reality. We no longer could commiserate over a cup of coffee, I could no longer talk to her about her times at the University, or share her exploits as a mother and wife, or listen to her ambitions. All of that was gone—lost.

What remains is the past: what was, not what could be. Death kills the evolution of relationships and the potential they might hold.

I read Betsy's note, just quoted, often because it sparkles with a moment when, by chance, I called her just at the right time as she was studying in Aix-en-Provence. Her voice and energy over that long-distance phone call made my day and hers, too. Small things, like a perfectly timed personal phone call, make a tremendous difference in our lives and often blossom into large, lifetime memories.

Paradox is an element of relationships. Although they are sturdy and can withstand thunderbolts, they are also fragile and can succumb to the delicate chords of dissonance. We don't always realize the impact we have on people, even on our own children. Our daily routine diverts us from expressing what they really mean to us and how our emotional connection to them gets us through each day. When the bond is broken, however, we are thrown into chaos. Death isn't the only relationship breaker; sometimes our own behavior and actions create a rift that ruptures and devastates relationships.

Five years before Betsy died I lived in Vermont. I was driving to the Dartmouth campus in Hanover, New Hampshire to have dinner with my friend, Ellen. We talked about life and I told her that things can get tough professionally. As we were driving, I told her that I got through some very difficult times.

I shared that when I was a school superintendent, the high school associate principal was shot to death in school while classes were in session. I received a call just before two o'clock in the afternoon that he had been murdered by a deranged 21-year-old former student. Less than a year later, I was divorced, lost my job, was scandalized by an affair, and moved "out East."

"I got hit by the Mack truck of life. First, the tragic, shocking murder was devastating. But, with the divorce, I actually ran myself over! I lost everything. Family. My daughter. Job. Christ, my self-respect. Nothing can sting more than self-destructing as I did."

"Well, you seem to have gotten through all that pretty well," Ellen replied. "Look at where you're at. You created a successful business and you made new associates and friends. Besides, you're respected in your field."

"Yeah, but I'll tell you, it was difficult and without people like you, I don't think I ever would've made it." I looked at the white frozen winter terrain and the beauty of the Vermont hills. We rode silently for several minutes and I said, "After those losses, I think I can confront anything life can now throw at me." Little did I know, hubris dies on the sword of reality.

After Betsy died, I thought back to that afternoon in Vermont and thought what a fool I was. Today, how naïve those words seem—so stereotypically macho and tinged with survival hubris. I'll take the loss of a career and reputation anytime, compared to having to face another March 9th.

I didn't take a hit from that Mack truck—it was a freight train. Betsy's death was in an entirely different league. No tougher one exists, except the loss of an entire family. Since that time, I've been a bit superstitious about saying anything about losses for fear that a tsunami of pain is just beyond the horizon. My ego's wings have been clipped very short, and now I look both ways for trucks— or trains. The realization that "it can happen to you" does that very well.

When I moved out East, I started a new life in Connecticut, then moved to Vermont for two years, and then back again to Connecticut in 2000. I spent many, many hours alone, finding my way around, trying to make acquaintances with colleagues. Actually, I was hanging on for dear life by a slim thread.

My motorcycle was my companion and obsession. I got lost all over the state and New England. Loneliness was my riding companion. One Saturday, I got up early, jumped on the bike, and headed west to nowhere in particular. I worked my way down to Fairfield County and headed east on the back roads adjacent to Highway 95. Suddenly, I felt isolated, separated from everything familiar and close.

I panicked to the point my heart was beating, it seemed, at the speed of a hummingbird's. My breathing became shortened, like I was running up hill full speed for five minutes. I had to talk to someone who cared about me, and who was grounded in my history and my past life. I stopped at a gas station off Highway 95. The traffic was whizzing by and the sound of tires on the hot pavement, racing engines, and bad mufflers added to the discomfort of 90-degree humid heat.

I found a pay phone and called Curtis, 900 miles away in Milwaukee—"Curtis, Dad." I said in a quick choppy cadence, my chest heaving with anxiety.

"Dad? What's all that noise? Where are you? In traffic?" Curtis said. He seemed to sense from the tone of these two introductory words that something was wrong. "Are you OK?"

"Yeah," I paused. "I'm OK. I'm driving all over hell. I really don't know exactly where I am for sure or where I'm going. I'm just driving . . . driving with no place to go or anything to do." Hearing his voice and concern calmed me down. "I'm in Connecticut . . . drifting . . . a bit lost, I guess."

"Chrissakes, Dad. Don't get in an accident—get hurt. Take a break. Get off the road, get some coffee or something. You got a map?"

"I'm okay, Curtis. Yeah, I have a map. I know where I am but I'm just lost. I just needed to talk to someone. Just a bit lonely," I didn't want him to worry, so I ended our brief conversation with some humor, "I'll be okay. You know me. My demons travel at 65 miles an hour and I can go 70 on the bike."

"OK, but be careful. Call me when you get home," he said. My heart slowed. The call felt good, my fear of total abandonment dissipated, and I misted up as I reached for my helmet and sat on the bike a minute, letting the miles catch up to me.

While traveling and seeing local and regional historical sites, like Newgate Prison, or the Long Island coastline, I would notice families snapping pictures. I became somewhat of a voyeur, observing with a bruised heart parents and kids being together as a family and sharing an experience. I told my good friends from back home that I became Connecticut's "man behind the camera," taking family pictures for complete strangers.

As their shutters snapped a pictorial record of the day, I would ask if they would like a picture of the whole family. For a brief moment, being the "man behind camera," I made a slight connection to others. They generally accepted my offer to snap a family candid. I always ended this brief interaction with "enjoy your family time together." The loneliness created an ache in me for the past when my family and I were in front of the camera. Memories of the times in Washington, D.C. or Canada rushed to the surface, along with snippets of family wisecracks and humor from those trips.

For a long time I lived with the illusion of control. You know, leaders are supposed to make things happen. Maybe that comes from running organizations, making decisions, collecting data, and measuring strategic gains. But in reality, I wasn't in command of much, and non-rational events forever altered my life. Irrational is the wrong word. Non-rational made more sense. I just couldn't understand why things happened as they did. Life is more complicated than a simple rational or irrational dichotomy to events. Non-rational—the events were simply beyond my understanding.

The outside world of work and my profession dominated my life. I worried about passing $65 million dollar budgets in the local community or dealing with complex programs and organizational issues, contracts, politics, and policies. They soaked up mountains of mental and physical energy, causing me to lose sight of what is important. Work is significant, but I learned that it is not essential to a fulfilling life. Leading an organization can provide a different kind of satisfaction, but one I would give up in a second if I could have averted the damaging hurt of betrayal and divorce. I couldn't see that I was out of control, but in quiet times, I could feel it. I have no excuses. I made mistakes. I own them and I am sorry.

Fairy tales don't exist. Things—sometimes ugly things—happen and contort our lives and relationships in new ways. We don't have a choice but to confront them.

Betsy's death numbed my spirit: actually, almost destroyed it. Friends could not lift the sorrow or even soften its hard edges. Reviving a petrified spirit isn't easy. But they stood by me, so I could lean on them and find strength in their compassionate energy. They didn't have to do anything or say anything except to "be there"—to care. Having a friend sit silently next to me was all that was necessary. Compassionate presence is powerful and immeasurable.

I realized the importance a single loved one can have on the meaning and purpose of life. In the hundreds of routine days, we don't grasp the role others play by providing the love and acceptance that we need in our search for a sense of place, belonging, and efficacy.

The corollary to this is that we don't fully recognize the influence we have on our children. We are too close to them emotionally to see our relationship with them clearly. We don't know how they perceive or value our interactions. If we are lucky, there are stories or letters and notes that give us a glimpse of how they sense and interpret us and our values and behavior, complete with our quirks and eccentricities.

Betsy's Valentine's Day letter that she sent to us during her first year at the University of Wisconsin is a treasure because she defined the small things that made us a family and were indicative of a place called home. When we received that letter, I thought it was "nice." In retrospect, it is an invaluable gift from her heart, complete with a little irreverent humor, using first names and all.

Dear Mom and Dad—"Mary and George":

When asked to write a "Valentine message" I thought back on the past 18 years and all of the special times. Our family trips to Washington, D.C., Boston, and Maine are still very vivid in my mind because they were always so historical and enriching.

Dad—Mom and I are still waiting for that vacation on the white, sandy beach next to the ocean (no thinking needed!). I also think back to the many dedicated hours you both gave to my skating. The practice sessions, the competitions, and the cost of equipment I thank you for and will always appreciate.

These memories have always been very special to me but since I've come to Madison I appreciate and think about them more. I miss Curtis' never ending alarm in the morning, the hockey games with the men of the family, and water aerobics with Mom. All of a sudden these trivial things become very important and are to be cherished and in my heart forever.

In these last 18 years, you have both filled my heart with love and security and each of you always gave me strength with your constant support so that I could achieve all of my goals and dreams. I thank you for this and for being the *best* parents a kid could ever ask for. I'm very proud to be your daughter.

I love you both very much!!

Happy Valentine's Day!!

Your daughter,
Betsy

I didn't realize it at the time, but Betsy was teaching me a lesson. Expressing the importance of a relationship to loved ones while they are still here is a timeless gift. Inevitably fate intervenes and the moment will be gone. We sometimes just assume life will go on as it always has and tomorrow will be much like today—a wishful fantasy really. A day that can change everything may be just around the corner. Mortality confronts us all at some point, and can strike with unexpected speed at an unforeseen place.

Children, however, have an innocent sense of wisdom about them. A friend of mine says that children are close to "the source." Maybe so. I don't know. But I do know that Claire has staggered me with her wisdom at times and Luke speaks truth with gentle bluntness.

On the day Bill was getting remarried, I drove Claire to the beach house where the wedding was being held to get her hair fixed and dressed for the occasion. My daughter had been dead for just 21 months and I was getting ready to see her father marry someone else. So, so strange, I thought, I was not at my daughter's wedding, but now I am witness to Bill's re-marriage. It was a difficult day, a strange day—an out-of-place day.

As we were driving, the fear of losing my connection to Claire and Luke overcame me again. I feared I might somehow be out of the picture—a remnant of the past and a living testament to a tragic, sorrowful day. That fear swirled in my head and tightened my chest. I didn't know who these strange people were who were coming into the kids' lives—I didn't know their values, history, or relationships. The fear made me verbalize my commitment to "being there" for Claire.

I turned and looked at her in the back seat and said, "Claire, I want you to know one thing. I will always be there for you. You can always count on Grandpa."

She sat silent for a few seconds. Then in a very soft voice she said, "What about D . . . E . . . A . . . ?"

I was caught short. I realized she was spelling "dead" or "death." I said, "D . . . E . . . A. . . . ? Oh, Claire, Claire! You don't have to worry; I'm going to be around for a long, long time."

Claire faced the loss "that lasts forever"—the death of her mother. After my comment, I realized that she seemed to know that relationships are not forever.

I think it was a strange day for her, too—it certainly was for me. She was very brave that day and I was never quite sure how she felt about her father getting remarried. I wanted her to feel support and comfort and to reiterate my love for and commitment to her—to let her know that I wasn't going to disappear. I guess I also needed to hear that, too, maybe even more than Claire.

When I was her age, I didn't want my mother to date anyone, and I certainly did not want her to remarry. I clung to my mother and did not want an interloper to change our family situation. I was fearful then, too, that my mom's love would go elsewhere by having a "stranger" come into our home. Actually, I was terrified the two times I remember my mom going out on a date. I didn't understand the fear. I just didn't want anything to happen to my mom that would disrupt our home and the routine certainty it provided.

With Betsy's death, the family culture and traditions in which Mary's and my grandchildren would be raised changed. No small thing! Many unknowns and ambiguity. Our daughter had created a wonderful vibrant, creative, and loving environment for Claire. Luke and Claire are not to have the benefit of that upbringing. The values, principles, and traditions that our daughter was raised with are more difficult to transmit to our grandchildren.

Mothers—women—are not interchangeable parts. Having another woman in the home does not produce the same result or culture that is so important in raising children. The family dynamic is altered. Someone else will be raising our daughter's children, bringing their own values toward people, education, duty, and life itself to bear on them. We didn't really know Heather. She was an unknown. Anxiety and concern cloud rationality.

I continue to fear, at times, losing my connection with my grandchildren. They live in Florida and I live in Connecticut, making consistent presence difficult. I didn't want Bill to see me as an obstacle that would strain our relationship over time. In small ways, the altered connection is evident as the pictures of my grandchildren on my refrigerator age and are not replaced regularly by new ones. Betsy sent pictures of Claire often and kept me in the loop of her life. Fewer phone calls and less communication create a weakened bond to my grandkids' everyday lives, because it's through the small incidents and activities of life that family ties grow. As a consequence, my dedication and determination increases, and I make regular trips to Florida to solder my connection.

In the immediacy of the death, the family—Bill's and ours—pulled together as a whole. We spent time helping the kids, filling in the gaps, assisting Bill in small and large ways to get through those difficult times. I delayed business and scurried to Florida whenever I could to support Claire and her father and to get to know Luke. We felt our family was tightening, despite the distance, but a sense of that connection was weakened sooner than we expected.

Certainly, Bill had to face the difficulty of being alone and raising two young children. The shock of finding out that he was dating about seven months after Betsy's death was difficult; not because I wanted him to live the life of a monk, but because I love him. I knew he was going to find someone—he's smart, principled, good-looking, and a very loving father. In a sense, I also felt I could lose my son-in-law. But the fear of the possibility of more losses is revived by small and sometimes innocuous events or words.

Moving into a relationship after the unexpected death of a wife and mother is dangerous territory. Some said it was good that he was "moving on." Information about the new liaison was dribbled out in bite-sized pieces and the flow seemed a bit manipulative. Bill cautioned us about how important his relationship was and that, in essence, Mary and I should not upset the apple cart. I guess Bill had worries, too, and I think, in his own way, he was trying to be sensitive to our sorrow. Loss creates difficult and sometime anxious emotions and scenarios for everyone. Fear is a real obstacle.

As grandparents, it was difficult for us to openly express our feelings for fear that we could lose contact with our grandchildren. We didn't want to offend Bill or his soon-to-be wife. The onus was on us to reach out and be hyper-sensitive to the feelings of others.

At the wedding, as Betsy's dad, I was in a delicate position—a part of the family, but not really. It was a Twilight Zone of sorts. I was a link to a heartrending time. I was caught between being a close acquaintance and a family member.

Few people can understand the feelings involved in being at a ceremony that is joyous and happy, yet mired in a quietly pulsating and very personal heartache. Another paradox. Like the collision of birth and death, there are paradoxical contrasts of heartache in such an event of heartfelt expression of love.

A new, blended family took the place of what was. Stepbrothers, stepfathers, stepmothers, step-grandmothers, step-grandfathers—all become intertwined in some new confusing dynamic. Different backgrounds and expectations came into play. Holidays and vacations had to be addressed. Visits to the grandchildren were planned ventures into new territory—when to come, where to stay— the familial comfort of the past evaporated. I thought, if

I'm confused, it must be confounding to Claire and Luke, especially Claire: so much change so fast.

Betsy's absence eliminated the spontaneity of going to Florida after only a quick phone call. Visits became a more formal act of asking permission. Talking directly to your daughter is far different from speaking with your son-in-law's new wife. Now measured tones and walking on eggshells are more prevalent. A father can say things and be more direct with a daughter than with a son-in-law's wife—if that is the accurate term for this relationship. How does one build a bridge to a person who is following a ghost and forming a new family?

All of this can be misunderstood. Some will say I was clinging to the past and not getting beyond Betsy's death. Getting beyond a daughter's death? People do not really know the pain—they don't know how I feel. They can't, unless they experience it. You never get beyond the death of one of your children.

I had to deal openly and honestly with my grief, the new dynamics and relationships, and look to the long-term. Removing Betsy from Claire and Luke's daily family picture was heart wrenching. God, I missed her. I thought I was going to explode.

My focus was on the children. I knew that life after Betsy's death was different and that Bill would find someone new over time. I knew that Claire and Luke's lives had been forever altered, too. But the way the aftermath of a death is handled is very sensitive to everyone so that changes do not feel like more losses and communication does not feel strained and misunderstood.

Honoring the past does not mean living in it. Creating a new reality requires that no one feels like a defensive victim. When it comes to understanding the delicateness of life, death is a blunt, powerful teacher. Lessons, however, are not always easy to learn.

Missing You

Missing you,
particularly things others don't notice—
things unique to you and me
so subtle that others can't see them.

Your smile is locked in my mind's eye,
along with the passionate energy,
bordering on intensity,
when issues raised the ire in your heart.

Missing you
has slowed my days in the quagmire of thought,
in the dark evenings of my heart. I
work the shadowy zone, where pain
moves in slow motion
with undulating acceptance.

At times I sit in disbelief
rubbing my hands, wondering
how and if this really happened.
Then, I snap-to and move my feet,
step-by-step to the next life task

trying to remember how it felt
before you left.

Missing you
has changed my life
because a part of me—
those parts of me I see in you—
also died;
breaking the human, genetic link and
the invisible ribbon of love.

So you're gone,
we wonder where you are, what
it feels like, whether you can see us,
if you're happy—
and peaceful.
We have so many questions. And,
only you know the answers.

Missing you
seems selfish and self-centered
and it expands,
like a massive cloud,
looming overhead,
of unresolved longing.

I fear as time goes on
I'll miss you less and
I fear that you will be angry and
think our link was loose
and inconsequential.
Guilt rears its ugly profile.

Missing you
has staggered my gait,
soured my confidence, and
raised my desire
to leave too. Only your spirit,
nurtured by memories
keeps me strong.
Your life still nourishes mine.

≈ 8 ≈

Memories

There are things in life that we must endure which are all but unendurable and yet I feel there is great goodness. Why, when there could have been nothing there is something. There is this great mystery. How, when there could have been nothing, does it happen that there is love, kindness, and beauty?"

—Jane Kenyon

On November 3, 2003, I received an e-mail from Betsy. "Thanks for everything you do for Claire; she loves spending time with you. I'm sure she is already looking forward to your next visit. She says to tell you, 'I really, really love you!'"

Years ago when Betsy, Claire, Bill, and I were having dinner at a Chinese restaurant. Claire, who just turned four at the time, never ate Chinese and was trying to manipulate her chopsticks. She wanted to try them, so she and I wrestled with those sticks and finally got her little fingers tenuously situated in position. Small hands, long sticks! Betsy brought some food for her to eat, including black olives which she loved, if she didn't like the restaurant's food. So we tackled the olives. To her amazement she focused, biting her lower lip in concentration, and to her and everyone's surprise she picked up that black olive sitting on her plate without stabbing it! She gave out a hearty laugh, put the sticks down and turned to me cupping her hands around my ear and said, "Grandpa, I love you." My heart soared! I can still feel that tender moment squirreled away in my heart.

I responded by countering, "I really, really, really, really, really love you, Claire." Since then, whenever I leave, it's a running joke between us. Luke, when he was six years old, topped it all once after I gave a six "really love you" goodbyes by saying, "I love you as big as the world!"

You can't top that! We don't forget those things and neither do the kids. My memories with my grandchildren shine exceptionally bright now because I realize the runway of my life is much shorter. Little connections we frequently take for granted have so much more meaning than before.

Memories never sleep. They dwell in perpetual insomnia. Small things spark them into action. Hearing a particular tune, seeing a Christmas ornament, driving behind a Toyota SUV, or just seeing kids carrying figure skates creates a burst of emotion and feeling for me. Even the sounds of cold steel on ice bring back a flood of memories of Betsy skating and our drives home together after a two-hour lesson.

One little nudge and the resurrection of feelings and emotions jump to life. Like a hologram of the past, you can see and feel the times but can't touch them because they reside in the subconscious mist of our memory.

Memories highlight joyful and light moments that, in many cases, were unplanned, unscripted, and unforeseen—significant because of the closeness and synergy they created. But some memories have a denser texture because they were born in those uncomfortable moments when misunderstandings or behavior shook faith and trust. We all experience both. We can only recognize, appreciate, and learn from them. They are what they are and cannot be erased.

Memories of sad times can shatter our rational façade with emotion and panic—smothering our sense of peace and serenity and shading our lives with melancholy.

Life Force

What comes of life?

Where does the energy go?

Our bodies, frozen in nothingness,

Rigid, silenced in death, lie

Empty of the life force that lights

Our hearts and feeds our souls.

Where does it go?

Where does it go?

Deeply sad and tragic moments live actively in my mind and consciousness—the horrendous murder of a colleague at work and the unfathomable death of my daughter. I can recollect the smallest details, the exact time things unraveled, and the physical feeling of those times—the shortness of my breath, the pressure on my chest, and my mind blurring confusion. That moment when Curtis said, "Betsy's in trouble and might not make it" still haunts me.

Sight produces powerful images. I remember looking at Betsy's lifeless empty and flaccid body, lacking the spirit that so filled her presence. Her hair spread out, uncharacteristically so. She didn't look like herself. Her indefatigable and unexplainable spirit was missing. Maybe that is all our bodies are—rented shells inhabited by our spirit on a short-term lease.

Remembering that haunting moment, standing in the darkened stairwell, when Bill told Claire that her mother had died creates a sense of helplessness that still tightens my chest. Even as I write this, the emotion of that moment resurfaces. Hearing her soft whimper was heart crushing: I felt so terribly helpless being unable to protect my granddaughter from death's hurt and pain. Sometimes I wish those memories would sleep. But ironically, my love for Betsy, Claire, and Luke keeps them awake. These memories have impact because they are tied to a broken heart.

> *The heart hath its own memory, like the mind.*
> *And in it are enshrined the precious keepsakes, into which*
> *is wrought the giver's loving thoughts.*
> —H. W. Longfellow

In reality, we wouldn't want to suffer amnesia from these memories. Our memory harkens back to how much we had that maybe we were not wise enough to appreciate at the time.

At times, unfortunately, I took my relationships for granted, never thinking that someday would be the last day I would see my son or daughter. Maybe we shouldn't think that way, but when life turns on you, you do. Memories, wrapped in the shroud of regret, brought that home too late. I certainly don't take anything for granted now. I try to be dutiful and conscientious to my son, wife, grandkids, and their families—otherwise I may lament again lost moments and opportunities.

Paradox is a part of living. Irony shows its face in so many places and in so many ways, with its unique twist of ideas and events. Inconsistency, not consistency, seems to be an absolute—the natural order. Control and certainty in life are fantasies.

Joys and pleasures are often underscored by sadness and pain. That's the paradox. Through life's losses and aches come renewal and growth. We learn and gain insight from both joyous and sad times. Wisdom does not always come comfortably, but can also arrive on the heels of grief and hardship.

Living means risking love—the deeper the love, the more profound the happiness or pain. Sadness and love are two sides of the same emotional coin. As Claire learned, sorrow is the opposite mirror image of joy. But love is the one thing in life that grows when you give it away. It is not a zero sum emotion. Love is also a gift we receive in the form of memories from those who've died—a gift we remember and can share with others.

But there's another paradox here. Death teaches us about living: it reminds us to examine and renew our commitments to each other. It stops us so we can see more clearly who and what is important, discriminating the true and valuable from the temporal and trivial.

Like everyone who has lost a loved one, I wished I would get a sign that she was in the proverbial better place and at peace. I guess we all desire a last indication and validation of their love and that there is something—some power and energy—on the other side.

A week or so after she died, I was talking with Peter, my neighbor, in the driveway. The cool twilight was getting grayer when there was a panicky rustle of birds tearing into flight from the flowering crabapple tree next to the stone wall. Peter looked up and shouted "An eagle! An eagle! I haven't seen an eagle on the farm in years! Wow, did you see that?" I saw the flash of its wings as it sailed upward over the corner of Peter's house. We stood there reveling in the unexpected sight.

Peter, who was raised on the farm, loved watching birds and could name all of them by the sound of their whistles and calls. We spent a few more minutes talking about the rarity of the eagle, and as the chill of the evening swelled, I headed to the house. I took off my jacket and went to my office to check my e-mail. While I was sifting through the spam and business stuff, to my surprise, I found an e-mail from Bill. I generally did not get much e-mail from him, so I anxiously opened it. He had written a short note about going to the golf course with Claire and letting her help "drive" the cart.

Bill was in charge of golf operations there and he wanted some time alone together with Claire so she could have some fun. He said he took some pictures of her driving the cart. By each picture, he wrote a brief sentence. I opened the five pictures and there, on the fourth slide, was a stunning picture of an eagle sitting on a branch, majestically looking to its left. He said they stopped and took this picture because Claire was excited to see it so close.

I sat back completely stunned. What are the odds that they would see an eagle on their trek around a golf course the day before I saw the rarity of an eagle on the farm the next evening? A sign? Coincidence? I don't know, but I like to think it was more than chance. I needed something and there was a synchronous sighting—a rarity. Was the eagle a reflection of her spirit? If so, it was an accurate reflection.

To me, it was Betsy's spirit, free from her body, letting me and Claire and Bill know that there is something beyond the hard, cold, vacant body she left behind. I called Bill immediately and he, I am sure, thought I was a delusional bereaved father grasping at a coincidence and giving meaning to it beyond reality. He is a man with a big heart and a very rational, linear mind.

Well eight years later, on my granddaughter's 12th birthday, I got a picture from Bill's wife, Heather, of an eagle sitting on the roof of their house. An eagle . . . on the house roof . . . on Claire's birthday. Another sign? Or just another coincidence? I know what I think.

When the pain of death subsides, we have to protect against falling back into the coma of earning a living, chasing brass rings, and the lure of gross materialism. Life really is about appreciating every moment—the birds, flowers, clouds—and the opportunity we have to be together in relationships with those we love.

In crisis or tragic times, we let down our defenses and façades and respond in genuine ways, exposing our emotions and beliefs—our true selves—not fearing vulnerability, but embracing it. We experience a sense of safe, mutual connectedness through compassion and empathy. We become joined in community in the best sense of the word.

In the immediate aftermath of the funeral, a "field" formed around our family and friends that connected us in an aura of emotion and commitment. It was Field Theory at work. It was just us—a family and friends—linked by a common devastating experience and by our mutual sorrow. I felt safe to cry, express disbelief, fall apart, or reminisce and share stories. Barriers were nonexistent, posturing was gone, and phony pretense evaporated.

Openness became evident and I had small, intense conversations with others in which we not only listened to each other, but also heard the beliefs, values, and emotions behind our fears and feelings. All Americans had that feeling after 9/11—we were all Americans linked and unified. The same happens in families and communities during crisis or during very special times.

The question is: how can we confront the inevitable losses, defeats, and deaths we suffer? In a real sense, life is learning to say goodbye. Everything changes; nothing is permanent in life. We move from childhood to youth, then to adulthood, and finally to old age. Our relationships with others and our understanding of ourselves are all that matter.

Each time we say goodbye in life we can wake up to what is important. Tears we feel are droplets of love as we let go of the moment and move ahead. They help us appreciate the wonder of it all—relationships, nature, and the seasons of life.

Someone once said that suffering is the price we pay for our humanity. We are the only creatures that laugh and cry. So, whether in happy or sad times, we must love each other, show compassion for others and ourselves, and rejoice in being alive and being able to feel. That is human and good.

The tears of grief and sorrow are tributes to the people we lose: we can use those tears to share our love and kindness with others, and in that way, we can pass on a part of the character of our loved ones that resides within us.

Your Dress

I hate to admit it because it always seemed curious to me when other people said they did this after a loved one died. But I smelled the black dress today that was hanging in your closet, hoping to get one more physical sense of you. Pictures are one thing. But your dress contained a very unique essence of your being emanating from the selection of perfumes, blended in a one-of-a-kind way with your skin and all else ever so slowly coming from your pores. I smelled your dress today—searching for one small morsel of your physical existence.

~ 9 ~

Forgiveness

The ring begins as a part of a dream
that buries me in fantasies and
nightly illusion.

Is it part of the reverie of sleep
or reality barking at me to respond?
The clock reported 3:50 a.m.

Like a retort from the past
the shock of the ring reverberated
in my chest—a testament to
history and anxiety.

Scrambling, dazed, the phone falls silent—
no message.
Was I dreaming or was it a psychological
flashback to March 9, 2004?

That fateful call at 3:50 a.m.

filled with panic,

desperation, and urgency,

signaled the start of the dance with death.

Why does the phone ring?

Or is it a dream?

Who's calling?

God, is it you calling

to say you're sorry?

Death strikes a new reality with overwhelming implications and consequences. It seems arbitrary: fairness is not a consideration. Death ambushed me and I was angry. It felt like an assassin's bullet struck without warning.

Initial disbelief melded into the clichéd anger of "What did I do to deserve this?" and from that came the search for who was responsible. How could my daughter die giving birth to a baby in the United States of America? Something must have gone wrong. Mistakes must have been made. Who was culpable? People were incredulous that this even happened because it was so rare and unusual—amniotic embolisms are uncommon and extraordinary but are also fatal or extremely debilitating. How could this happen? It just doesn't happen here. It shouldn't happen here.

Even though shock numbed my body, when I arrived at the hospital, I was strangely lucid and rational. I realized I had to get information to find out what *really* happened in the delivery room. In my job, I was accustomed to dealing with legal questions of proper and ethical conduct, supervision, and appropriate practice.

I also knew the hospital administrator probably called the lawyers early in the morning to alert them to Betsy's death. Despite the complimentary turkey sandwiches, coffee, and soft drinks, I was sure he was concerned about legal action. If he wasn't, he wasn't doing his job. While our family was sitting together in a cocoon of numb emotion, he was probably having a rational, strategic exchange with his attorneys about possible malpractice liabilities, timelines of events and procedures, pertinent data and records, and getting written statements from all those involved and present.

Acting quickly, I thought, was essential before the hospital staff could adjust and cover up. I told Curtis "we have to get information before the administrator tells the nurses and others to shut down, if he hasn't already." While many of Betsy's friends were taking care of Luke, Curtis and I headed to the nurses' station and asked for the names of all the doctors, nurses, and staff present at the time Betsy died, how long she was in labor, the name and contact information for the hospital administrator, and what other individuals were present during the delivery.

While cursory, I wanted details about the people who were there. I did this under the guise of wanting to send a "thank you" for their assistance to Betsy. Manipulative—yes. But I thought it could be essential to find out what happened. I've found that in tragic situations, I place emotions on the shelf and coherently try to gather information and facts. I couldn't believe my daughter had just died, we had just returned from seeing her body, and I was acting like an executive facing a crisis. I guess some behavior doesn't die easily.

"Curtis, you have to sit down and take notes about what was said to you and at what time. You were here when Betsy died—you and Bill—and and I think you should write a chronology of who spoke to you, what they said, and the time they said it. "We have to get as much information as we possibly can because we have to find out what happened to Betsy and why," I said.

He, too, was focused, "Dad, I'm a cop and I've been in a lot of emergency rooms. I don't know if they were really prepared for something like this . . . they were running around like chickens . . . getting more blood and things. The very young doctor, I think, was there when she died. I think the older doctor wasn't present when things started to go to hell."

In several days, he sent me an e-mail:

> 12:55 a.m.—The doctor came out to update Bill. . . . There were complications with procedure and [she] explained about being unable to stop the bleeding. She said, "We might lose her."

> 2:00 a.m.—Numerous nurses running back and forth. She's in serious but stable condition.

> 3:15 a.m.—A doctor came in and asked Bill for permission to perform a hysterectomy. Bill said, "Yes!"

Roughly 4:00 a.m.—The young physician said that Betsy was in serious condition, that they were still breathing for her and it would be touch and go for a couple of hours. She said that Betsy was going to be taken down to the intensive care unit.

A few minutes later—Dr. _____ came in and said that Betsy was probably going to die. She explained that they are breathing for her and when they stop, she doesn't maintain breathing and blood pressure.

Betsy died. 5:15 a.m.—As I walked out of intensive care I was met by the CEO of the hospital . . . and he gave me his card and said if I needed anything to let him know and he would take care of it and that he was sorry for my loss.

To some, my actions may seem cold and calculated in light of the tragedy. But in reality, I was acting on a pledge I made to Betsy when I was flying to Florida—that I would find out what happened, why, and who was responsible. I had to find justice for my daughter and for my grandchildren. Betsy was gone, but I made that promise to her. But the road was not without obstacles.

As Betsy's parents, Mary and I had few legal rights. Bill was responsible legally and had control over any recourse. I vowed that I would do a thorough job of finding out what occurred. I also had to do this for myself in order to come to grips with what happened, and as her father, I really had no choice. It was the right thing to do. I wouldn't find peace otherwise. Uncovering the truth and the circumstances of why my daughter died giving birth to Luke was my parental duty and obligation. Betsy would do the same for me if circumstances were reversed. She had a great sense of justice and I could do no less.

Some weeks after the funeral, Bill's friend, who is a lawyer, suggested an attorney who could look into the case. Mary, Bill, and I met with him, along with his attorney friend. Before we got started, I asked, "What experience do you have with medical malpractice law and cases? I know these issues can be complicated." He replied that he handled several cases, but that malpractice law was not his main focus, since he had a small law firm. He then went on and explained the legal requirements needed to prove malpractice. I made it clear that money was not my motivation. Justice was. I wasn't going to degrade my daughter's memory by making this about cash.

The attorney suggested that an expert review the documents because that would give us an indication of whether there was "a case." He rightly indicated that proving malpractice is difficult, which is contrary to public perception.

Because I had dealt with many lawsuits in my past, I said, "I would like more than one expert opinion. I know there are people who will give you the opinion you seek. I think if there is a case to be made, having two independent experts review the materials separately and arrive at their conclusions independently would strengthen our case." The room fell silent.

I felt some reticence from Bill about this. He nervously rubbed the side arms of his chair lightly with his hands in response. I could tell this was emotionally difficult for him. I said I would pay for the second opinion because "I have to know," what actually happened.

The attorney looked at me a bit surprised. I said that as her father I needed this in order to heal from the loss.

That was the truth, but the calculating way I expressed it put him in a position where he had to agree. I emphasized that I would do anything to find out the truth.

To this day, I don't quite understand the unspoken, quiet tension that I felt between Bill, Mary, and me around looking into malpractice. We were all devastated by the loss. But the three of us rode down the elevator in silence. Was it grief? Reliving the loss? Control? Fear? Guilt? Maybe the pain of it all? Maybe not knowing is comforting and relieves the responsibility to act. Or finding out that people's actions caused a death might make it too hard to bear. I don't know. For me it was plain and simple: justice. Was her death providence or human error or negligence?

An amniotic embolism? I had no idea what that was, what caused it, or why it was rare. All I knew was that it struck out of nowhere and that Betsy was gone. I had to find out more, in addition to taking a legal path.

I talked with a child psychiatrist at Yale about Claire and Luke and the loss of their mother, as well as the issues I was facing in light of it. I asked him about amniotic embolisms and he recommended I talk to a research physician at Yale who was knowledgeable about these issues.

I called the Yale researcher and he said that these embolisms are rare, but deadly, and cannot be anticipated. Medical texts do not have much about them, maybe a paragraph or two, because there are not enough cases to do a comprehensive research study. Anecdotal cases are all researchers have.

He explained what happens with these embolisms, using the metaphor of aluminum Jiffy Pop popcorn pan. After 25 minutes on the phone with him, I got a better understanding of the devastating impact this amniotic fluid has on the lungs and brain of the mother and how it surges into the bloodstream. I learned that predicting an amniotic embolism is difficult. There are very few, if any, signs, and once in the bloodstream, the fluid, most frequently, is deadly. Monitoring its occurrence can't be done like observing the patterns and rhythms of a heart beating and functioning. Understanding this helped me comprehend what occurred and its implications.

When I got back to Connecticut, I asked my neighbor Peter, who was also an attorney, if he knew of any good malpractice lawyers. "I have to work with this attorney from Florida whose main experience is not malpractice," I said. I had to pursue this situation in more detail "just to be sure" that the conclusions are correct. He recommended a friend whose major practice and expertise was medical malpractice. She agreed to see me to discuss the process and laws concerning malpractice. This was a stroke of luck.

She reiterated the difficulty of proving malpractice: her firm takes maybe ten percent of the cases presented to them because proving whether the physicians involved did not follow the "standard of care" is complicated. She was very compassionate and professional. I finally felt comfortable with her expertise and judgment. Although she would not be an active lawyer in the case because her firm was not licensed to practice in Florida, she said I could meet with her with my questions about the process.

After several weeks, the external reviews were completed. When the experts gave us their opinions separately, the one chosen by the Florida attorney presented a general overview that I felt was not sufficient or comprehensive. It became clear to me that my strategy for a second expert opinion was a correct one.

The second expert provided a more precise and comprehensive review of his findings via a conference call. I was in Connecticut, Mary was at home in Wisconsin, and Bill and the expert were in the attorney's office in Florida. I was able to ask many questions and he provided detailed answers. I asked him if he reviewed all of the materials that he received from the hospital physicians and he responded affirmatively. He also highlighted specific areas of significance in a case like this.

My gut told me I had to see those records. So I asked him if he would send them to me so I could put my mind at peace. My tone as Betsy's grieving father was a bit manipulative, because legally I had no right to those records. He asked for my address, and remarked that the autopsy records might be difficult for me to see. I thanked him and said, "I appreciate the conscientious review and detail you provided to us."

So that was that. For Bill and Mary, the conversation seemed to have closed the case. But I was not finished. When the records came in a large, sealed manila envelope, I couldn't open it for several days. It was too emotional. The package was substantial and heavy. I finally opened it and had my first view of the official record of the events of Luke's birth and Betsy's death.

I quickly reviewed the autopsy report. The devastating record for me, however, was the electrocardiogram of Betsy's heartbeat—her dwindling heartbeat reduced to a flat line caused my heart to race, and I broke down and sobbed holding this narrow paper record of the last trickle of Betsy's life. Of all the records, the electrocardiogram illustrated her pathway to death clearly and unequivocally.

I took the records to the attorney in Connecticut and asked if she would review them. Was another opinion in order? She knew we had two expert opinions and didn't think that another would change their conclusions. But she said she would review the records with an attorney's eye for any red flags that would raise any questions about the viability and accuracy of the records.

At our next meeting, she reported, "from a records standpoint, things seemed to be straightforward. No red flags." I thanked her for her time and compassion. She was helpful on many fronts. Her objectiveness and professional grace provided a sound foundation for me in my search for peace. Going to those great legal lengths was predicated on finding justice and peace of mind. I could not move ahead with unanswered questions that would follow me to my grave.

Sitting on the sidelines and letting this pass would have haunted me. I had to find out the truth to the best of my ability. This was not the time to settle and then live with regrets later.

All families face issues of righteousness at one time or another. I wanted Claire and Luke to know that I and Mary and their father did everything possible to seek justice for their mother. I knew full well the magnitude of the loss to them. When they are older, I want them to know that I am a person of my word and that they could count on me even when faced with resistance. There are times in life you have to stand up, even when others disagree, to pursue issues, to do what is right, and to find peace. To me, this was obviously one of those times.

Justice and peace are intimately connected. When bad things happen beyond anyone's control and are not of malicious intent, we can live with a peaceful heart understanding that the mystery of fate intervened. I could not live with the doubt and regret that I did not answer the call and make sure that this is what actually happened. When grief engulfs us, it takes courage to act, question, and explore options, particularly in difficult or unpleasant circumstances.

In the emotional heat of Betsy's death and the subsequent examination of legal issues, I needed a refuge—a place to go to be alone in solitude, away from *doing* to just *being*. A small, wonderful, stereotypical New England church in Milton, Connecticut, served that purpose for me. I came to this church to sit and think, and also to do some writing. Although I was not a member of the congregation or even a churchgoer or a true believer, my neighbor Eileen was an officer in the church, and she got permission for me to sit and write there.

The light coming through the stained-glass windows was bright and the energy was positive and uplifting. The quiet and solitude were peaceful. This little church became my sanctuary in the true sense of the word; it was where I could be alone and find myself.

I needed a meeting with myself. There are lessons to be learned by spending time alone. Religion was not the purpose: sanctuary and contemplation were. This is where I came to grips with forgiveness.

To forgive is a lesson in life I continually have to learn. After Betsy's death, I thought, why this happened particularly, as I looked at others whose lives seemed whole, intact, and normal. I still yearned for the customary family life and relationships I had in the past. I didn't feel normal and feared that I might never attain normalcy again because things seemed twisted, surreal, and unjust.

Forgiveness is difficult—and very misunderstood. We confuse it with other things like condoning, ignoring, excusing, or seeking compensation for hurtful acts.

Forgiving is not approving, forgetting, or overlooking wrongful acts. Nor does forgiveness concern being morally superior and granting others absolution from above. Forgiveness is a much bigger idea.

Forgiveness is needed when people hurt us, when losses happen, or when we lose a sense of ourselves. All of these are great issues. To a degree, I felt all of these losses. We want to put things back in order—to gain a sense of wholeness again in our relationships with other people and ourselves. Of course, I wished nothing had happened and that Betsy was still there. I still do. But wishing is just wishing. There is no magical thinking with death.

Even though I had the legal opinions, there was a hollowness in the process and a disconnect from the people who were actually with my daughter at the time she died. My first reaction was retribution, which usually ends up creating a cycle of revenge. Anger is a natural emotion that can cloud our visions and minds and can affect our rational and moral judgments.

The legal process seems fractured, creating distance between people—specifically, between Betsy's doctors and me. Distance is difficult and generates suspicion and animus. I thought, my daughter died under their care and I can't talk to them?!?

My time in the Milton church, alone with my thoughts, readings, and writings, helped me resolve those splintered feelings. I had to forgive myself in some ways for the five years Betsy and I were estranged, and I had to forgive others, too. A lot of water went under the bridge, and I had to come to peace with it all.

Forgiveness, I learned, could make things whole again—maybe not exactly as they were, but clear and open, without the negative residue of resentment and fear.

Forgiveness was the answer to inner and external peace, to feeling whole again, and to being able to forge new relationships with others. It does not mean approving of bad behavior or hateful, despicable acts. Rather, it means looking ahead and not living in the past by having those acts haunt us in every aspect of our lives. Forgiveness was essential for me to move ahead as healthy as possible.

Forgiveness is an act of courage, not a sign of weakness. It is an antidote to anger and fear, both of which can dominate and control our lives. Bad things inevitably happen in our lives. Letting tragedies control us destroys us and tears at our spirit and optimism. All great religions speak of forgiveness for this reason. It is essential to forgive to free us to fulfill the promise within us and to live a happy and meaningful life. Unfortunately practicing forgiveness isn't easy.

Acting with goodness—with empathy and compassion—requires turning to the better angels within us, and not living in the dark shadows of resentment. Fear drives out love and lets ambivalence, anxiety, and guilt take control and direct us. Forgiveness is a highly moral act and is necessary to live with a sense of goodness, virtue, and caring. Love and peace can only come through forgiveness.

Forgiveness is a twofold gift. First, it shows the goodness of the human spirit to another person. Second, it offers us the gift of healing. Striking back, seething, and hating can only be destructive to our health and character. Retaliation breeds retaliation. Fighting fire with fire is destructive and noxious. Forgiveness changes the fabric of a relationship resurrecting a sense of wholeness.

We cannot move ahead with our lives if they are cemented to the past, glued to our errors, or defined by our disappointments and brandish old hurts. To live in the present moment is to forgive those who hurt or disappointed us. We cannot let people who injured us occupy space in our heads. Nor can we relive, over and over again, our past errors and the guilt associated with them. Guilt should be felt, because it is the voice of conscience, but it can destroy your life if it eats eternally at your spirit and confidence.

As a consequence, I had to take one more step and speak directly to Betsy's doctors. Malpractice was no longer an issue. That process really doesn't help with healing because it seems so impersonal in one of the most personal tragedies one can experience. I wondered if Betsy was just a case number, an incident that unfortunately played out in tragedy.

I had to look into the doctors' eyes, the windows to their souls, and communicate directly to them about Betsy's last moments. If I could see and talk to them, then maybe I could move ahead knowing they did absolutely everything within their power to help her.

I asked if they would meet with me. The Connecticut attorney said, "don't be surprised if they say no or cancel. Their attorneys will not want them speaking to you." I decided to try anyway, and to my surprise, they agreed. I contacted them personally by phone and asked if they would be willing to meet with me and talk about Betsy's death.

I needed to know more about the "rare" amniotic embolism, which was the cause of her death: why and how the amniotic fluid entered Betsy's bloodstream. Little research exists, the Yale expert said, since the number of cases is not large enough to provide meaningful hard data, just anecdotal incidents.

The medical review did not resolve my feelings that exploded within me with Betsy's unexpected and sudden death from a procedure that routinely and joyously occurs thousands of times a day. I wondered about how the physicians reacted having a person die under their care under the circumstances. The way I saw it, that pain tied us together as human beings. That's why I decided to talk directly with Betsy's doctors—with no pretense, no physician-patient roles, no legal formalities. I needed to see and hear directly from them that they did everything they could.

But Betsy's doctors did not cancel.

We met on the patio of a coffee shop near their office. I think we were all anxious. I could feel my heart beating in my chest while waiting for them to arrive. The younger physician, who was Betsy's age, 34 years old, arrived first. We hugged and I could see the tears well up in her eyes. The senior doctor, wearing her "greens" arrived directly from the hospital. Her walk seemed heavy and cautious.

We found a discrete table, away from the crowd. At first, they appeared tense and uneasy. We sat quietly for a moment and then I said, "You know, we looked into malpractice. This isn't about that. It's about a father's need to find resolution." Each replied softly that they couldn't fathom how devastating this was for me and my family and that it was overwhelming for them, too.

"I need to know how this happened," I asked quietly. The young doctor related the chain of events that led to the crisis. She said the delivery was difficult for Betsy. When the baby's heart rate indicated that he might be in distress, they decided to do a Caesarean section. Everything looked fine at first, she said, until they pressed on her stomach and found she was bleeding profusely internally.

She looked down at her lap and her voice quaked when she said she had done everything she could. The incident haunted her. With a quiet intensity, she said that she had replayed the situation over and over in her mind, and that ever since Betsy's death, she second-, third-, and fourth-guesses herself in dealing with her patients to ensure she covers all the bases. She actually questioned whether or not she wanted to continue in medicine because of what happened.

I could see the pain in her face. I sat silently and asked, "Has this ever happened before?"

The senior doctor, who had more than 25 years of experience, said she had seen nothing like it in all the time she had been in practice. It was a rare circumstance, she said, very rare. She paused and looked at me intently tears were beginning to fall from her eyes. She put her head down on the table and wept.

She stammered softly that Betsy was a beautiful person who always brought such light and energy to the office and made friends with everybody there. She said, "I had had more than a doctor-patient relationship with Betsy." She shared that she delivered Betsy's first child and helped her through two subsequent miscarriages. "Everything had looked fine with this birth," she said.

The human-ness of that moment moved me to ask about Betsy's last moments. Having heard her first cries, I needed to know about her last. I wondered if she had suffered, if she had known the end was near. The doctors said that Betsy wanted to know how Luke was. The last thing she heard in her life was that Luke was healthy and fine.

Our meeting together was tender and caring. We held each other in a spirit of compassion when we were parting. I fully realized the extent of their sorrow. Hearing their assurances that they had done all they could felt as though two sides of an open wound had been stitched together, allowing the healing process to begin.

Betsy is gone. Her family and friends feel the loss. I miss her every day. The void is great and, at times, dark. But I had kept my promise. Justice is not always found in a courtroom. And peace never is.

⌐ 10 ⌐

Hearts

Betsy had a generous heart and infectious spirit that touched the lives of all who knew her.

—Great Grandmother Meyer

The Soul

The soul stands alone

Separate from the gray

Light of thought.

Blanching against reason

It echoes the past,

The time before we arrived

In our bundled blankets.

The soul is the heart's

Reflection,

The synchronous partner,

The soft receptacle

of intuition and wisdom.

135

We live in such a cognitive, rational world. Metrics, it seems, rule accelerated by our confidence in science and the glitz and speed of technology. We live in an era where a scientific story is playing itself out nationally. We seem to have physics envy. Numbers, graphs, polls, procedures, and standards all emanate from the altar of measurability. Some people feel that if it cannot be seen or measured, it does not exist or is of little consequence. In our work-a-day world our rational minds are supposed to govern our behavior. The head rules. Emotion and intuition are mistrusted.

With life and death, however, love, not metrics, matters. Age, dates, or accumulated wealth are meaningless: what remains are intangible feelings and the immeasurable outpouring of love. Death has massive power, but it is love that breaks hearts. They rupture because of the explosion of our love for the person who is gone.

Living is not about arithmetic, calculus, or data. It is about matters of the heart, which speak with more clarity and simplicity than our heads. Our hearts have to do with being, not analyzing. They concern relating, not rationalizing.

When Claire asked the question about whether our hearts were heaven, maybe she was right. In an innocent way she believed people when they said that her mother would always be in her heart. I know Betsy dwells somewhere within me—why not my heart?

All of us have a longing to belong—to be loved unconditionally with compassion and acceptance. Hearts are tangible organs, but they are also metaphorical symbols of the spirit and soul that resides in all of us. Our souls are what are left when the world scrapes away our façade, our earthly titles and positions, and our outward selves.

Tragedies, loss, and death have a way of skinning us down to our common humanity.

We can learn from our children. On a trip to see my grandchildren, Luke, who was six years old and in kindergarten, spontaneously looked at his father at the dinner table and said, "Dad, I love you." In his innocent way, he uttered simple wisdom and truth: an earnest and spontaneous expression of his love with no self-censoring and no self-consciousness. I am continually amazed at how children help me see life with the fresh eyes of innocence and confirm their love unconditionally through the grace of simple words and touch.

Why do we hesitate to say what's in our hearts and express it to others? Do we think the timing isn't right or are we trapped in our façade and image? Sometimes, I think our so-called social values constrain us. But when people are gone, we yearn for just one more opportunity to say, "I love you." The panicked phone calls the 9/11 victims made to spouses, children, and family members were made in a last, desperate effort to say, "I love you." They made no mention of material things or jobs. Just love— one more time.

One of Betsy's friends wrote me a note about a book she received from Betsy during the Christmas holidays in 1997. The inscription read, *"For we must always remember we are unique and on this earth for love and kindness."* I cherish that quote and have it posted on a wall so I can remind myself each day. We all need those sentiments and must not forget their value to the people we love and honor.

The heart speaks to us in different ways, sometimes in optimism and at other times with an aura of concern. Expressions of love have a heartening effect on us. They encourage and nurse our spirit in tough times. Sometimes we even have difficulty with expressions of joy. It is easier to find comfort in our cognitive side. Many men have this difficulty, I think.

At times, friends have said, "Jesus, George, you get too emotional. You know if you want to get ahead, you have to mask your emotions. You're too passionate. You can't show your feelings." Indifference, I thought, rides on the shoulders of dispassionate silence.

The word *heart* has many extrapolations that are particularly pertinent in difficult times. There is nothing counterfeit or artificial about these expressions, and when we receive them, they are truly gifts that last forever.

I can trace the *heart* stages that I experienced that dark day—March 9. The first call from Curtis about Betsy's condition was troubled but *heartened* because the doctors were pursuing a different medical procedure to help Betsy. Although he did not use that word—heartened—I felt a glimmer that the ordeal was going to end positively. The glimmer, however, faded with a second phone call telling me to get down to Florida as soon as I could.

Instantaneously, I became *heartsick*—that sinking feeling that things were not moving in the right direction. Heartsickness weighed heavy as my heart beat faster and with deeper intensity, a reaction to impending difficulty or struggle. Hearts do more than pump blood; they intuitively sense the energy of possibility or tragedy.

When Curtis told me Betsy was in serious condition and close to dying, my heartsickness became *heartbreak*. The loss was so deep that my world stopped and my heart fractured, taking away my breath and disorienting me physically as I literally walked in circles. A cascade of my unconditional love for Betsy and the inability to express it to her directly any longer caused the heartbreak. I seemed to be bursting inside . . . and I still am. The pain of heart-break may diminish, but it never really stops or goes away.

Broken hearts create an outpouring of absolute love. In a strange way, that outpouring transports us to when we were children—free to express genuine, unfettered emotion. I know that I should have expressed those emotions more frequently with simple gratitude to people when they were alive.

Death freed my heart and now I convey my love to family and friends, and even my business partner, Lou. When he was sick and for the first time in our business relationship and friendship, I said over the phone, "I love you, Lou." I learned this lesson the hard way: if I didn't say it now, then when?

Death exposed my essence, crumbling my veneer of competence and exposed my vulnerability. I found myself in the well of deep passion and feeling:

- Passion that overwhelms

- Passion that rides at the surface

- Passion that is pure, honest, and open

- Passion that comes from the depths of our souls

- Passion that is evident without regard to circum-stances or venue

Curtis' eulogy at Betsy's memorial service was filled with emotional fervor for his sister. We remember things because they are *heartfelt*—expressions of deep sentiment. Although Curtis was not known as a person to stand up in front of hundreds of people to give a speech, that heartfelt passion rose to the surface in a spontaneous and extemporaneous outpouring of love for his sister. Passion flowed from his soul and rushed over the audience, capturing them in the warmth of love as if an invisible force field engulfed us.

Love and Sorrow

Love and sorrow are two sides of the same coin.

One's sorrow is in direct proportion to one's

love for another when they are gone.

I am thinking of you in this time of unrelenting sorrow

in celebration of your beautiful and endearing life.

Sometimes there is no tomorrow, as the poet Jane Kenyon reminds us in her famous poem "Otherwise." Death does not wait, and time does not matter.

Another illusion concerns time. Time does not move in equal increments in real life as scientists attest. I realized that after Betsy died, those years we had together seemed to fly by in a flash. Special moments we shared arrived unexpectedly and did not have to last forever to become significant and precious. Those extraordinary times in the car driving to her skating lessons or meeting at the University of Wisconsin or sharing her nervousness before a skating contest, while brief in terms of minutes, have significant power for me. They last forever.

We all know, however, that in times of despair, the minutes seem to drag into torturous hours. Loneliness slows time to a crawl, and with it, the emotional pain can cause the clock to stop. A friend told me that Einstein's theory of relativity could be defined by our experiences. In joyful times the clock moves rapidly, and in those difficult situations, we feel like we are sitting on a hot stove with each excruciating second moving at the pace of a snail on Valium.

I also learned that being present with those we love is the one gift we can give them and ourselves. Being *present*, sharing and devoting unobstructed moments with a person, is one of life's greatest gifts because it dignifies the nobility of that time with them and is respectful and loving. We only have a limited number of moments to give in life: share them with those you love, if not in person, then through a hand written letter or note.

As I get older, I value those times:

- When I called Betsy from Vermont on a cold early spring day after years of separation, and she said, "Hi, Dad, what are you doing?" just like old times, as if the harsh times of estrangement were wiped from memory.

- While driving in Florida with my son-in-law, Claire and I sat in the back "jump seat" and she grabbed my hand and held it for miles and miles.

- When Luke and I hook our little fingers together as a special greeting or when he is feeling sad and needs a sign of care and affection.

- Sitting together in the car, when my wife Marilyn, Claire, Luke, and I all joined hands and sang "It's a Wonderful World" along with Willie Nelson.

- When Bill speaks from his heart and reveals a bit about himself and the responsibilities he faces.

- When Julia and Eddie, Curtis's children, jump up and down and wave when I pull into the driveway.

- When Luke, Curtis, and I go to Chicago for a Black-hawk game—just the guys.

I think back to those times as exceptional because we were all focused and present, recognizing our connection to and affection for each other. We all long for those moments of closeness.

Broken hearts can bring people together. Some have supple hearts—broken but able to produce the capacity for healing. Healing is not easy; it hurts and takes time. But some people's hearts can turn brittle and shatter into pieces, impossible to put back together. The toxins of anger and cynicism inoculated them against the joy of love.

The love, joy, and happiness we experienced together is the salve to rejuvenate our broken hearts. We must not wait for the unpredictability of fate to bring us back to the innocence of expressing genuine love and affection to those close to us and to humanity in general. Isn't that what we all desire and need—to find peace collectively and personally?

An Innocent Moment

I saw this little girl from afar standing
in front of the post office with her father,
and I was taken back to
another time so many years ago.
A time when life's ebb and flow
circled around our family routines
immune to the coarseness of life
and the spectrum of loss.

The innocence of the girl's image,
open to the present moment just
standing in quiet spirit with her dad, and
the unknown fate of her life.

You leapt from that glance
to my heart filled with memories
of times past, when that same
peaceful innocence embraced us too.

I know now that the cold
winds of life can create a shiver in
our hearts as the unexpected face
of mortality breaches the innocence of life.

⌒ 11 ⌒

Goodness

I am very open and approachable, making others feel comfortable around me. One of my favorite things to do is to sit down and talk and learn about other people.
—From Betsy's University of Wisconsin application
for foreign study

As a parent, I wanted Betsy and Curtis to be good, but I did not mean being a 3 on a 5 point Likert scale between excellent and poor. Goodness is deeper and more philosophical than a vacuous numeric rating scale. Mary and I wanted them to have a sense of "goodness" about them in their decisions and their behavior. We knew that how they were going to live their lives depended on character.

When they were children, I would tell them that they were not "special." Many of my friends were aghast at that. "How could you tell your kids that they are not special? My kids are!" I always replied, "Don't get me wrong, I love my kids. But I want them to understand one thing. There's a difference between being special and being unique. My kids are one-of-a-kind. Distinctive. Precious. But so is every human being and each person should be honored and respected. If I tell them they are special, then they think they are better than other people." Elitism, to me, always had no place in a diverse world.

On one of our rides into Milwaukee for her skating lesson, Betsy and I passed a woman standing waiting for a bus on a biting, windy, stark, drizzly, November day. Her coat was shabby and she was holding two full plastic shopping bags and had a plastic babushka on her head to protect her from the mist. Betsy, who was about nine years old, said as the bus was pulling up, "Dad, look at that old lady standing on the corner. She looks poor."

"Yes, she might be, Betsy. I want you to know one thing though. You, that woman, and I are cut out of the same cloth. All people are. Because we have a car and a nice house doesn't mean we are special or any different from anyone in this poor neighborhood. Everyone deserves respect and dignity. Don't ever for a moment think that because people have money, fame, or material things they are more special than others."

I got philosophical with my kids at times even though they would sometimes roll their eyes in aggravation. After a while, they came to expect it.

Betsy looked at me quizzically. I knew the wheels in her head were turning, so I added, "If people believe they are special, then they think other people must not be. Specialness divides people. Some people think they are better than others. Because you are popular doesn't mean you have a leg up on those who are not. You are unique and that lady on the corner is unique, too. All of us are distinctive in our own ways and that is something to be cherished and celebrated. Remember, there is no royalty among people—there are just people trying to live their lives as best as they can. We are all connected. And we end up with the same fate."

Today, our society is enamored with so-called idols, superstars, and celebrity. It seems sick to me that as a society, we fall to idolatry and royalty and social standing. In many cases these so-called special people are hollow.

Our society and media push the message of separateness by highlighting celebrity, promoting false idols, and focusing on red carpets. Substance succumbs to the superficiality of the glitz and manipulations of Madison Avenue and Hollywood. False hierarchies are touted and some "prominent" individuals believe that rules do not apply to them. Privilege, under any pretext, is toxic in relationships and our society. Deviance and egocentric behavior are highlighted and the common person is inundated with the exploits of the so-called super stars and wealthy class.

I was never sure whether these little lessons were fully understood by my kids. I wanted our children to have the values and principles essential to being a "good" person: an individual with empathy, understanding, compassion, and genuine humanity, with the character to lead a purposeful, meaningful, and constructive life.

When a person dies, their character is all that remains and what people remember. It comes alive in the experiences and stories people tell about them. I guess Betsy learned that lesson because she was transmitting those values to Claire. According to her good friend, Tami, she was driving to Miami for a children's concert with Betsy, Claire, and another friend and her two daughters. In a letter to Claire and Luke, Tami wrote this anecdote about their mother:

> On our way back from the concert, we got stuck in traffic in Miami, maybe even a little lost. At one point, we found ourselves in a poor neighborhood.

And while we were inching along in stop-and-go traffic, we saw several men standing and sitting around one run-down building.

Claire asked, "Mommy, what are these men doing out there?"

I was glad this was not directed to me and I could pretend I was driving. How do you explain to a 3 1/2-year old child about the misery of homeless people and failure of society on their part?

And then came your Mom's answer: "Claire, Honey, those men do not have a home right now, so they are looking for a place to spend the night, get a shower and maybe a hot meal. See, not everyone is as fortunate as we are to have a house to keep us warm, a bath to keep us clean and a Daddy who works to buy us food. But that does not mean that these are bad people. They are God's Children just like you. . . . Maybe you could say a prayer for them tonight at bedtime so God will help them."

What compassion and love your Mom had towards people, no matter if she knew them or not, no matter in what fashion they crossed her way.

Betsy was not perfect—she'd be the first one to say that. But when she was in high school, I saw her goodness when she brought home a foreign exchange student at the beginning of her senior year. As a junior, she met Silvina, a Rotary Club exchange student from Argentina. She was at a party and noticed Silvina off by herself standing alone. Betsy went over to talk to her and then realized that she was one of the exchange students at her high school.

At the time, Silvina couldn't speak a lick of English! With Betsy's limited Spanish, they communicated the best they could. When she got home, she was excited to tell us about Silvina, and asked if she could invite her to our house for dinner.

The next weekend Silvina came for supper, and we went to a University of Wisconsin hockey game and then for a root beer float at Mullin's Dairy on the way home. In spite of the language barrier, we all connected; Curtis, Mary, and I used a lot of sign language and smiled a lot, and I found myself talking louder, as if that would make English more understandable to Silvina. This was a new and fun experience for all of us.

Betsy and Silvina became like sisters and, as luck would have it, the Rotary Club was looking for a host family for Silvina for the second semester. Of course, with my daughter's urging, our family offered our home. Silvina lived with us that year, sharing a bedroom with Betsy, and became an integral member of our family. She is still part of our family today. Hosting an exchange student was a wonderful experience for all of us. Little did we know that a chance meeting at a party would develop into a lifetime bond.

Silvina was a joy to our whole family. We learned about her family and we got a view of America's influence in the world that was much different from what is reported on television or offered by so-called pundits. I am proud that Betsy lived her life in such a way that it represented her very "being" and character. Her compassion for people was a characteristic her friends valued.

One of her principals in high school wrote, "Betsy taught me that I should be more careful when dealing with people's emotions." She stood up for principles even with her principals! That is why she became involved in several issues at school, including revamping the graduation ceremony.

Betsy served on a committee of five seniors and three parents to review the graduation ceremonies and make them more dignified and less raucous. She was interviewed in the newspaper about the committee's work and what can be done to improve students' behavior at graduation. Betsy spoke up and believed that the best way to combat the problem was through peer pressure instead of administrative mandates.

She was quoted in the local newspaper, "the majority of kids want a formal ceremony and, for students our age, almost anything can be changed with peer pressure. This is our chance to go out in style, to be different from previous classes and show the community the class of 1988 can handle the ceremony."

Betsy disagreed with some parents who wanted students to "let loose" if they wanted. Betsy said, "They don't have the right to decide for me and the other students who want to remember this day as a formal event." The committee's work was a success.

At times, today's world makes it difficult to be optimistic. The news and the media are filled with travesties and violence; even children's so-called entertainment is filled with brutality, vulgarity, retribution, terror, and fragmentation that dehumanize people.

Raising our kids, we tried to emphasize that people are basically good and that goodness surrounds us. Philosophers debate the definition of goodness. Certainly following a moral and ethical course is "good." If our actions have integrity to high principles, then we have a sense of goodness. When we treat others respectfully and act peacefully toward people of the world, and when we recognize and dignify others as equals, then we act with goodness.

Doing good is one thing but *being* good is another. The *being* requires introspection and self-knowledge and goes beyond the shallow world of roles, materialism, and social position. *Being* comes from within us, is part of our soul or essence and portrays who we really are. Being an ethical and loving person who acts peacefully and with fortitude defines our character. Ideals such as honesty, integrity, humility, acceptance, and openness come to mind.

I made mistakes, some of which hurt others. I broke a vow and felt repudiation, even by my own family. Betsy's initial rejection, as I have said, was tortuous for me. In a way, I totally understood her denunciation. I fell off a pedestal children sometimes put their parents on. I too hated myself for the destruction of a family and my career and public trust.

Somehow, through meditating, reading, and study, I came to realize that I was not the worst thing I have ever done. That sounds easy, but not for me. I am a no-excuse type of person, and the fact that I did wrong, ethically and morally, caused me to fall into personally rejecting myself—anything else I did in my life did not matter. My "being" was crushed.

Only after isolation and some depressing moments, did I realize that my whole being could not be reduced to the worst thing I ever did. Eventually, Betsy came to a similar conclusion, after 60 long, difficult months. When my affair became regional and state-wide news, I hurt Mary, Curtis, and Betsy. Seeing your father's name and picture on the front page of the *Milwaukee Journal*, above the fold, was devastating. Somehow Betsy eventually got to the point of realizing that I was more than a mistake and life is more complex.

After her call to me and subsequent discussions, I think she saw me more completely—not just as one decision. People are not perfect; they make mistakes and still have a base of goodness within them.

By acting with a sense of goodness, Betsy recognized that specialness has no place. Goodness opens the doors to others and recognizes their frailty and humanity.

Big Questions

The big questions in life

Come wrapped in simple covers,

Often unnoticed and invisible

Harking to the voices within us

That we have not heard or listened to

As we tread through the tangible world.

Like a time-release capsule, those queries

Fill our veins slowly, almost unnoticeably,

With the bittersweet nectar of change, flowing

Un-perceptively until, through spontaneous combustion,

Our masks melt and betray our childlike honesty that

Hid in the mind's inner forest, tied in the velvet chains of

The expectations and compliance imposed by others.

Breaking those soft chains is a silent act

Taking place in the placid ponds

Of mind and soul that erupts
Tidal waves coloring the world in
New and unexpected hues of passion.

That passion amends the eyes of others
Who now see you, unblurred by
False images and façades
Lifting the veil of approval that divides
And makes us noble mirrors of each other.

12

Meaning

I would trade places with you at that critical moment.
My life . . . what more can I do?
Yours . . . full of energy, promise, hope . . . love.
I wish . . . I wish.
　　　—Scribbled in a book jacket of mine three weeks
　　　　　　　　　　　　　　　　after Betsy died

Our hearts and souls do not succumb to clichéd reasoning. Analytical reasoning and religious belief are
inadequate even when cloaked in the best scientific or
theological explanation of death. When tragedy strikes,
life does not slide back to what was, continuing as if death
was simply a comma in the narrative of our story. The
trajectory of the story is knocked off course forever.

Every day, I still wish I could trade places with Betsy
for two reasons. I have had a full life, complete with
accomplishment and success, as well as defeat and failure. My life has been extraordinary only in the sense that
everyone's life is distinctive and exceptional. I had a good
run. What more is there? Secondly, I deeply wish Claire
and Luke had the opportunity to know their mother and

155

have the advantages of her profound passion for life and commitment to them. She was at the threshold of fulfillment and deep meaning, whereas I was reaching the hilltop gliding toward the inevitable end. Betsy was actualizing herself as a mother with her two children. But it is not to be. Her story is written in the past tense.

Philosophically, most people understand the difficulty death brings. People, however, cannot truly feel the slow dirge of pain and despair that parents feel with the loss of a child. Meaning vanishes and everything seems trivial. To think about the meaning of my own life while carrying the cold stone of Betsy's death seems impossible and, in many respects, dishonorable to her. I sat with the pain in order to accept its magnitude. Wishing it didn't happen didn't do a thing, and doing so did not help me move to acceptance. A wish is just an empty fantasy.

Dark Side of the Moon

You have to be on the dark side
Of the moon of your soul
To understand deep loss.

But memories are beacons of light
And warmth that cradle your heart
And caress your being

Calling you home to what is.

Time doesn't really heal: that old cliché falls far short of the gravity of the situation. For it to be true, we would have to erase all of our senses—our emotions, memories, associations, and the sight, smells, and sounds of things we shared.

Acceptance is an undervalued word. We speak of tolerance, but we can be tolerant through disdain or indifference. Acceptance requires coming to grips with situations, confronting and believing the reality of events with no magical thinking or delusion.

My mom used to say that "everything works out for the best." Her belief was probably a throwback to her religious upbringing as a child. But she also rejected religion as an adult after my father died leaving her with a four and a seven year old to raise. I wonder if she really believed in that saying or just said it with the hope that things would work out—with or without God's will. She really had no choice. Maybe it was just an act of acceptance, a "nothing I can do about it anyway" attitude.

Acceptance is balancing and understanding our being. Grieving is not simply a matter of doing things or going through structured phases. Cognitively I understood them, but emotionally and practically they were academic jargon. Resilience is essential because death threatens your basic foundation—your core. Life loses its luster, the myths of our childhood stand hollow, and the weight of sorrow makes Sisyphus's challenge minuscule by contrast.

Resilience requires being a realistic optimist. Realistic in confronting that Betsy was dead. But optimistic in confronting what I experienced and applying what I learned to living my life more fully and with a deeper sense of purpose. The adversity of death must be transformed into living with intention, committing to using my talents and abilities in a principled way, and seeking goodness in every day that remains.

The pain of death, however, can scar our souls into indifference. Love and sorrow are inevitable companions. Loving deeply resides in the same well from which our sorrow is drawn. Indifference is the opposite of love, as the author Elie Wiesel stated.

Our obligation, then, is to give meaning to our lives and not live in the cynical cocoon of indifference. My despairing response to Betsy's death is evidence of the love I felt for her. Finding myself in that anguish and moving ahead with my life in a passionate and purposeful way didn't come easily or simply because of the passage of time. Time passes, but it doesn't necessarily heal. In fact, I am still working on it, and when tragedies happen, I live the pain all over again.

Sometimes, the only thing that happens is time passes and we find ourselves in the same place but with a different perspective on our beliefs, motives, and truth itself. As T. S. Eliot stated:

> We shall not cease from exploration
> And the end of all our exploring
> Will be to arrive where we started
> And know the place for the first time.

Easier said than done. Exploring takes time, and we must take it to work through anger and fear. I was frightened. Struggling to find the resilience and move ahead was too painful. I just wanted to forget the world. Just curl up, purge my mind, anesthetize my feelings, fade away.

Finding ourselves sounds so vague, like it came off the cover of a pop psychology magazine. Losses, however, catapult us away from routine business as usual. The weeks after Betsy died were filled with activity: preparing for funeral services, dealing with cemeteries, responding to phone calls and notes, and so many other things that I cannot even recollect. People were always around and the only time I was by myself was in bed, trying to sleep, where I had to face the demons of regret, anger, and guilt. The cloud of night's darkness mirrored the darkness in my heart and soul.

After the flurry of activity, I returned to my home, to be alone in the old farmhouse and its original old wooden beams and floors scarred with tractor tire chain marks of times past burned into them. The rustic warmness of it provided positive energy and a sense of familiar comfort but also came with a quiet foreboding of loneliness and isolation. Knowing that Peter and Eileen were close by in the large farmhouse next door was comforting.

I feared living in isolation—aloneness required facing my feelings and new realities squarely. Being alone now meant my world had a different color and face, and it was darker, colder. I wasn't sure I could survive the loss by myself. Even though I was frightened of that prospect, I used the time to sit and feel the void of the loss and its wrenching heartbreak.

Being alone actually turned out to be a gift of sorts. I wrote poetry, listened to music, and explored religious books of all types. Poetry and certain books, particularly those that included letters of others in grueling, heartfelt situations, were the most helpful, in addition to the music of Copland, Grainger, and others.

Dietrich Bonhoeffer, the German theologian who was imprisoned by Hitler after the von Stauffenberg assassination attempt, wrote something that stayed with me.

It was about solitude. He wrote to his friend Maria von Wedemeyer-Weller,

> But I have had the experience over and over again that the quieter it is around me, the clearer do I feel a connection to you. It is as though in solitude the soul develops senses, which we hardly know in everyday life. Therefore I have not felt lonely or abandoned for one moment.

Solitude and being soaked in my sorrow helped me to see the connection between pain, suffering, love, life, and meaning. Solitude helped me, not totally, but to a great degree, to empty myself of fear, anger, and negativity.

As I thought about what Betsy meant to me, I remembered the goodness *in* and *of* her life. In those solitary moments I could feel Betsy's love, personality, and character. I realized there was a point where I felt I was becoming addicted to negativity and remorse; not only because of her death but also because of the five years I had lost with her because of my decisions that led to my divorce.

A master paradox: death creates rebirth. But a rebirth does not come without struggling, questioning, doubting, or anxiety. I learned that if I was to find meaning, I had to use my abilities to pursue what I loved in a consequential way. We all have a destiny to fulfill in life. We mustn't forgo it.

How could I squander the time I have left when Betsy's life was cut so short? I must live life fully and pass on the love of those who are gone to others: it is my obligation to do so. This was no heroic venture, but the only way I could see not to be chained to the past or to engage in so-called magical thinking. I had grandchildren who needed love and care. Life was precious and had to be lived with purpose, even when pain was a companion.

On one of my trips to Florida four years after her mom died, Claire—this effervescent, spirited, and dramatic little girl, who loves to dance, jump around, and perform—was called the drama queen during dinner. She was told to stop being so dramatic after she told a story with exuberance and inflection. After those words, she sat back and slumped in her chair.

Claire is vibrant: that is who she is and she has to live her truth and be her genuine self. We all must. She can't live a life to please others and not to let her spirit shine. I was silent, but angry, because I saw so much of her mother in her. I did nothing.

In a quiet moment later that evening, I whispered in her ear, "Claire, don't ever let anyone dampen your creative spirit. You are enthusiastic, smart, and expressive. Don't you forget that." Certainly I see a bit of Betsy's fervor in her, and I understand she has to be the person the daemon or genius inside her calls. She must find her calling and destiny. She cannot be what someone else wants her to be; besides, no one has that moral authority or right.

All of us have our own voice, just as she is discovering and testing hers. We have to use our talent and potential. We only have one life to live and we cannot live the life others want us to live to please them. I remember trying to be "good" as a child or later in life. When I first got a job, I did things with which I disagreed to win favor with another person. I had to learn that I could only give of myself in an authentic and genuine way—not the way others thought I should. I had to be my own person, even if that doesn't always please others.

Betsy was a natural. She was born to be a mother—that was her calling. In many ways, her life was happy. I could see the joy her experiences brought her, from her skating, to her time in Europe, to her marriage to Bill, and to the relationships she had with friends. Certainly the pinnacle of her life and purpose was clear in the birth of Luke.

She was content in her achievements at school. Betsy had mostly A's and a few B's in college. My son, Curtis, fondly remembers a time a month before her graduation from Wisconsin. One Saturday in May, Curtis, Mary, and I met with her for lunch at the Nitty Gritty, the same hamburger joint I took her to earlier in her college days.

Only once in her entire collegiate career did I advise her on taking an elective course. I suggested a course on organizational development, because I read the professor's book and he was very prominent in the field. What a great opportunity, I thought. Well . . .

The professor required two major assessments. One was a test she took in February in which Betsy earned a D+ [the only D she ever got on a college test], and the second was a final exam that was looming in two weeks. As we were sitting waiting for our order, Betsy said, "God, Dad, that course you told me to take is the worst. We listen to videotapes of that 'great professor' you told me about and then have to deal with graduate assistants. Laura and I got D's on the last test and now I'm worried about even passing the course. The final is in two weeks," she whined. "I need the credits for graduation!"

Curtis got this wry expression on his face and couldn't contain himself. He shot back, "Quit complaining. You can't take the pressure! I'm always on the cusp of getting a D or failing a course. Snap out of it."

We all laughed because Betsy was conscientious, structured, and, as her brother said, "totally anal." She was always driven to do well, and was a bit of a perfectionist. He, on the other hand, had a more relaxed attitude toward his studies. Conscientious, but with a "don't sweat it" attitude typical of a testosterone driven, eighteen-year-old male. Well, she passed the course with a B, but not without angst.

Looking back, I think her life was fulfilling. She had good ideals and always wanted to help others. While in high school, she worked for our neighbor Mr. Snyder, who had multiple sclerosis and needed assistance to do shopping, and some typing and collating for the business he had out of his home.

She had talent as a skater and a dancer, but she also had the knack for interacting and talking with all kinds of people and personalities. She used those skills for good causes: she used her creative imagination to teach children how to skate and she was a nurturing mother. She was a good friend and always reached out to people, particularly those in need.

As I think back on those moments of solitude in the little farmhouse, I vowed once again to live in the present with people, respect humanity, and treat all with dignity. I know it sounds trite, but a tragedy exposes very plainly what is important to keep clearly in mind every day. Even though I was 27 years her senior and her father, Betsy's life moved me to recommit to look ahead and live actively and passionately.

Silence

Silence does not wear a neutral face
It bears a quiet disguise
Borne of life and memories past.

A schizophrenic friend it is—
One that warms the heart
Or freezes the soul

Silence speaks in different tongues
In muted tones or the raging sound
Of a life lived to the hilt.

Silence moves on velvet slippers
Stalking our heart with chords of fear
Tying our minds with the barbed web of life.

Silence caresses in warm reflection
Bathing us in holy light
Letting us know that we are not alone.

≈ 13 ≈

Death

*Fundamentally we feel that we really belong to death
already, and that every new day is a miracle.*

—Dietrich Bonhoeffer

We come into the world alone and we leave it walking a solitary path. Death's presence is with us from
the time of our birth. We do not know the time, place, or
circumstance of when we shall die.

As there are cycles in nature, life has its cycles, too.
But the cycle can be uneven and abrupt, even leapfrog-
ging stages and expectations. We just never know when
the cycle is going to end. People we love die. Our pets die.
Organizations and companies die. And someday, we will
die. Death and pain are an integral part of life. Although,
if we live life and use our talents, when it's time, we can
caress the end in satisfaction and fulfillment.

No one is immune to sadness and suffering. In that
way, I guess life is fair. No one escapes pain. Nature, while
beautiful and splendorous, can also be devastating and
disastrous with its unpredictable force. Storms and earth-
quakes kill and alter people's lives in an instant, teaching

us very clearly that death's unlimited force is far beyond our control.

Actually, disequilibrium is the norm. The delusion of control is a fantasy. The only thing that we can count on is that nothing is permanent—certainly not life. We are taught early on to be in control, even though the natural world in which we live is impervious to our manipulations. We cling to the fantasy of our power and our penchant to "make things happen." Plans, goals, and objectives are made as if life is an exercise in engineering. Many will fall victim to fate or a confrontation with our own talent and happiness. As I have learned, death is quite an antidote to that figment of our imagination.

Youthful exuberance denies our inevitable mortality. Living in a cocoon of invincibility seems carefree, but eventually "the lonely visitor" arrives at our door. Wealth, power, friends, or fame are impotent to the "great equalizer."

Our mortality, however, should push us ahead to living with vigor and a touch of wild abandon. That takes courage. The prospect of death, in a way, should be liberating: after all, what is there to lose? What are we waiting for?

Individuals and our society generally have a discomfort with death and those who grieve. We use euphemisms as if they will protect us from the reality, as if death is contagious. We slip into terms like "pass away," "pass on," "expire," "depart," "loss," and "eternal rest." George Carlin would be proud. In a humorous, but incisive way, he would add: "check out," "buy the farm," "kick the bucket," "go to the happy hunting ground," "push up daisies," "go to the other side of the grass," or "sleep the big sleep," and more.

Death is not transmittable, just inevitable, and we should be able to discuss it without code words. On the other hand, when a baby "comes into this world" he or she is simply "born" or "arrives" as if by taxi or plane or the proverbial stork. Fear versus joy, I guess. Death, in some respects, is seen as an omen boding evil: the "kiss of death" or the "death knell."

The Wish

I wish I was with you

When the lonely visitor came

I hope you felt safe . . . loved, and

I wish I could've been there

To help you make the lonely transition

In a caress of comfort and love

Death is life's greatest mystery: its real nature is unknown to us. We only see the remains. Myths, stories, and parables describe the divine intervention and implementation of "God's will" as we engage in the journey toward eternity. Images of heaven and hell and even a fuzzy condition of purgatory are proffered as we turn ourselves over to a Supreme Being. All of this seems like such a fairy tale of primitive cultures with a limited and superstitious understanding of the world.

With Betsy's death, those parables rang hollow and raised more doubts than comfort. I didn't experience the Hollywood ending where a born-again epiphany of understanding happened and I fell into peace and grace. Far from it. Religious explanations or divine providence did not help. Maybe I have no faith or my spirit and soul was broken and faith vanished. Maybe faith doesn't have to be the result of religious dogma and teachings. Agnostics and atheists find peace without any deliverance experience or supernatural intervention.

The fact of the matter is we don't know what is on the other side. These parables and stories are supposed to give support by describing the better place where Betsy and others like her are supposed to be in eternal happiness. Religion extols death as a place of peace: you are going to heaven, you are being rewarded with virgins (another curiosity), or you are being next to God.

Forgetting

When I was born I started to forget ...

the angel pressed her fingers across my lips

and slowly, each grain of memory dropped

into the well of present reality

eroding the face of God and memories of home.

In learning about this world, I forgot

about life in the great beyond,

in the life before life

hidden in the mystical haze of eternal peace.

When I die, I will forget this material world
and remember, once again,
the life of love, stillness, and peace.

When Betsy died I felt helpless. There was no time to say goodbye. I couldn't respond or help her. I could only hope that she was free of pain. I wondered if she was fearful or died in the warm light of peace that the scriptures and other religious doctrine indicate are present at the time of death.

I wondered if she was aware that it was her time. To this day I think about how difficult it must have been for her to leave baby Luke. They were only on earth together for such a short time—minutes really. If she did know, that must have been a courageous act for her to accept leaving her children. Or maybe, she didn't understand that she was dying. Maybe the lights just go out? Is there a deeper intelligence and understanding? It's still a mystery; I wish I knew, but I don't, but one day I will.

Impotence is death's accomplice. The one thing we all share at the time of death is the powerlessness to stop it. I only hope that Betsy's passing from this world was peaceful and comforting to her.

I almost drowned once. I remember the initial thrashing around, gulping for air, and then after a few minutes I stopped struggling and a warm, comfortable feeling engulfed me; I seemed to be floating, unaware of trauma or the necessity to breathe. Only when a friend pushed me to the surface did I fight to save myself. Death didn't seem frightening and there was no comprehension that I might die as I floated beneath the surface. I hope for my daughter that warmth and peace were there for her.

Death impels us to recognize life as it is: full of joy and happiness, as well as pain and suffering. I understand more clearly than ever how closely our lives are bound up with other people's lives and that the center focus of our own existence is outside of us. In examining how we move through life, Bonhoeffer expressed:

> It is remarkable how we think . . . about the people that we should not like to live without, and almost or entirely forget about ourselves. It is only then that we feel how closely our own lives are bound up with other people's, and in fact how the centre of our own lives is outside ourselves, and how little we are separate entities.

Life requires courage on our part to love—to be vulnerable to the sting of death when we love with our whole heart and soul. Another paradox! Deep, comforting love is the source of anguish and suffering but also is the wellspring of great joy and happiness. To avert the pain, some people do not risk intimacy and turn to isolation and try to immunize themselves against sadness and loss.

We cannot let the pain cut us off from others. In a philosophical sense, we must be thankful for broken hearts because they are evidence that we found happiness in the love of others and had the courage to trust our hearts. This, however, is no simple journey.

The poet John O'Donohue wrote that,

> Grief is the experience of finding yourself standing alone in the vacant space with all this torn

emotional tissue protruding. In the rhythm of breathing, you learn to gather your given heart back to yourself again. This sore gathering takes time. You need patience with your slow part. It takes the heart a long time to unlearn and transfer its old affections. This is a time when you have to swim against the tide of your life.

Certainly, the continuity of our life is disordered and shattered into pieces. Healing a heart takes time and the fortitude to risk being vulnerable like that again.

When people die, the metaphor that they are going home is frequently used in poetry and, in my view, is the most comforting one. This too presumes something after death—a place our soulful energy goes. Going home? I don't know if she's "home," but I can only wish and hope that her soul and spirit are, in some way, part of the essence of the universe and her children.

Betsy's death left a feeling of absence that translated into loneliness. There are times when I wish I could have just one more hour with her—just one.

A Poem for Betsy . . .

Birth and death
Two sides of the same coin of life . . .

Today we celebrate your life,
Earlier this month we mourned your death . . .

The ying and yang of existence in this world

Brings the dense clouds of sorrow and
The delicate air of joy and exuberance.

Memories of your death brings both
Cold mist and warm light . . .
They, too, are two sides of the coin of love.

Missing you raises all the beautiful moments,
And all the energy and zest you brought to life . . .
Gifts from you to be enjoyed forever.

My love still grows for you . . .
Missing you . . .
Is loving you eternally.

Epilogue: What Does It All Mean?

Even a happy life cannot be without a measure of darkness, and the word happy would lose its meaning if it were not balanced by sadness. It is far better to take things as they come along with patience and equanimity.

—Carl Jung

Many books about loss, death, and the grieving process are on the shelves of bookstores. What to make of them was always hard for me to figure out, even though I experienced the death of my parents, grandmother, aunts, and uncles. The death of my daughter, however, was different: it wasn't her time. In my mind, it violated nature. Spring, summer, fall, and winter metaphorically describe the natural order. Betsy just got through spring.

March 9th is Luke's birthday and the day that Betsy died. The juxtaposition of death and life presented simultaneously was overwhelming and confusing. We tried to celebrate Luke's life, and we do very deeply today, but the sorrow of that day was overwhelming and it remains so. The sadness was also for Luke, of not being able to know his mother and all she had to offer—love, energy, optimism, enthusiasm, culture, and adventure.

Curtis once said, "Too bad they didn't change Luke's birth date to March 8th. He was born shortly after midnight on the 9th. At least then, his birthday would not be on same day his mother died." One day Luke will realize this juxtaposition. I hope he realizes the love Betsy had for him and feels secure in that thought. She wouldn't want it any other way. Fate intervened and both he and Betsy were its victims.

Death for children is an abstraction. They do not understand that it is absolute until after seven or eight years old. The child psychiatrist I saw after Betsy died said that we should answer children's questions as they are presented. To paraphrase what he said, "you don't teach children calculus before they understand numbers." Just answer the question without giving a dissertation.

I wonder how Luke will consider the circumstances. He is now aware that his mother is Betsy. When he was five years old, while we were blowing up balloons in the field by the side of my house, he asked, "How did my mom die?"

Taken aback, I didn't know what to say. I had no information about what Bill said to him about Betsy. I didn't really respond, boys his age are easily distracted, and we continued blowing up balloons. The question came out of the dark, and I wish I could've answered in a way that would respond and not create any confusion.

I learned that children comprehend more than we think. They are quite astute in feeling energy and piecing things together. Curtis said that when Mary took Claire and six-year-old Luke to the cemetery to visit Betsy's gravesite, Luke said, "That's my first mother." He realizes that Betsy was indeed his natural mother, and Heather, who he calls Mom, is in his life, too. Maybe he put it in the proper perspective—honoring the past and the present.

While looking at the gravestone, he then asked, "Why is my birthday printed on the stone?" His grandmother replied, "Because your mother loved you so much." Luke, at six years old, is coming closer to putting the pieces together that she indeed died giving birth to him.

How to handle the sensitive issues is difficult. Although the psychiatrist's advice is just to answer the questions as they come up, it is easier said than done. The one question I still don't understand or know how to answer is, "Why did she have to die?" I don't have a good answer. And I never will. I just want Luke and Claire to be at peace knowing that Betsy loved them and that there was nothing that could be done to change things. They must celebrate life and live vigorously and virtu-ously—with principles. That would honor life, Betsy, and themselves.

All deaths are not the same. I was able to talk to my mother two days before she died and was able to say, in the course of our two-hour conversation, everything I wanted to tell her. I knew it was the last time I was going to see her. We reminisced, told stories of earlier times. I told her of my admiration for her courage in raising two kids as a single parent, and I also assured her that my sis-ter, Betty, and I would always be connected—that really was her last wish.

With Betsy, it was much different. After my mom's death, things got back to a "new" normal. Accepting my mother's death and being at peace with it came almost in a natural process. But with Betsy, it was different: more intricate, nagging, and catastrophic. Some of my friends said, "Give it time, be kind to yourself, and eventually things will get back to normal." Normal? Normality does not exist. Normal is what one wishes but that fate determines.

The Dark Hand

The dark hand
crept into our lives
and pushed us to the frontier
distant
from everything we've known
and foreign to our senses.

This inevitable
and seemingly arid frontier
where pretense is unknown
awakens
us to the beauty and sting of our existence
handed to us in unnerving and unexpected ways
pushing our humanity to its limits.

Living on this frontier of who we are
pulsates with fear and joy
simultaneously
in a curious paradox of
mournful remembrance and respectful celebration.
Dying begets living to its fullest.
We learn of ourselves at this place
struggling once again to find joy that fills
our souls

and breathes fresh life into our spirit

as we wait for the dark hand

to awaken us to life once more.

Well, it didn't exactly turn out that way. Nothing was
ever the same again. An emptiness, a void that could not
be filled, shrouded my thinking and experiences. It still
does. Betsy was a unique, one-of-a-kind daughter who
was just entering an important phase of her life, and she
was gone—cut down by fate. For me, going back to normal, back to business, would have been insensitive and
impertinent because that normal died with Betsy. I was
lost in the cacophony of feelings and the insensitive world
that got "back to business." I was, in a sense, floating.

I learned that by taking one piece of our puzzle of life
out, the picture changes, patterns shift, and relationships
are reworked in subtle but significant ways. Old relationships fade, new ones develop, connections to family members evolve differently, and passion for some aspects of
work dissipates as others grow.

The deep desire to help my grandchildren and to
remain an important part of their lives will never die.
The relationship with my son-in-law Bill is significant
to me and remains and has grown. He has been open
to my active involvement with Luke and Claire, and for
that I will always be in his debt. His goodness has been
so very gratifying and healing for me. My love for him as
he faced and continues to face this tremendous adversity has grown. And his new wife, Heather, was placed in
an extremely difficult circumstance: following a popular
woman who suffered a tragic death. Not an easy role.

Some dreams have slipped away too. I wanted to be a father to her and help raise the kids, by being the best grandfather I could be. I wanted to make up for the lost five years. Being separated from her still rips at my soul. We were weaving a new relationship from the strands of the past and the new realities we learned and faced. Slowly she began calling me and asking for advice. One day she called and said, "Dad, can you come down because I want you to see the school I'm thinking of sending Claire to." Being an active part of her decision-making about the education of Claire felt natural and good. We were back together—whole—as father and daughter.

Now, with Bill's blended family, it is more difficult because I don't want to overstep my bounds. Tender soil of a new family culture exists and I've learned to walk softly. Determining my role in that family is more delicate than before. I am simply "Grandpa G." who visits periodically and brings Claire and Luke up for an annual visit to the farm. Sometimes I feel like an appendage—a reminder of a sorrowful time.

There is no certainty in life. We are simply "beings" who have to address forces beyond our control and the order of things, natural or not. Finding our way in the world requires that basically we have to uncover and understand why we are here and our reasons for living. Facing and accepting ourselves can be complicated because of our aspirations and vulnerabilities. If we don't understand ourselves, we can get buried in an avalanche of grief and never find peace.

Life's only script consists of birth and death. We fill in what comes between. Life is not a mechanical exercise that follows an orderly path. Whimsy and mystery, serendipity and surprise fill our lives. The clichéd story of a main character succumbing to tragedy, falling into a funk, having an epiphany, and seeing the light and then proceeding back into normalcy doesn't really happen. Not for me anyway. Things don't settle back into "before" and we don't find a substitute for what is gone and absent. Finding peace takes time and is a creative process of small steps, plateaus, and setbacks.

Dietrich Bonhoeffer's letter from jail to his brother said it well:

> First: nothing can make up for the absence of someone whom we love, and it would be wrong to try to find a substitute; we must simply hold out and see it through. That sounds very hard at first, but at the same time it is a great consolation, for the gap, as long as it remains unfilled, preserves the bonds between us. It is nonsense to say that God fills the gap; he doesn't fill it, but on the contrary, he keeps it empty and so helps us to keep alive our former communion with each other, even at the cost of pain.
>
> Secondly: the dearer and richer our memories, the more difficult the separation. But gratitude changes the pangs of memory into a tranquil joy. The beauties of the past are borne, not as a thorn in the flesh, but as a precious gift in themselves. We must take care not to wallow in our memories or hand ourselves over to them, just as we do not gaze all the time at a valuable present, but only at special times, and apart from these keep it simply as a hidden treasure that is ours for certain. In this way the past gives us lasting joy and strength.

This passage rings true because the memories of Betsy and our relationship made it more difficult to deal with her absence. Past memories are a reminder of the joy I had watching her grow from a baby into a competent business-woman and a loving and nurturing mother and wife.

Time does not ever fill the gap—don't fool yourself. Although I remember the joy, I also know that there are no more memories in the making. I also know that I cannot make rational sense out of what happened. I just have to accept it and remember what was, take care of my grandchildren, move ahead in life, and honor my daughter's life and memory.

I shall not forget. Maybe our hearts are heaven: a place for sacred memories tempered by love and loss to rest and to help us continue to live.

Autumn of Life

I sit in the late autumn of life

With the stirrings of spring singing in my soul, oblivious . . .

Oblivious to the weathered image in the morning mirror,

And to the dance of time and the reality of age.

There are days when I walk on colt's legs

Prancing on spirited limbs, filled

With the vibrant smells of life,

The bliss of emerging potential, and

The dreams of races to be won.

I feel caught,
Suspended in the illusion of time
Attached to the innocence of the past
Yet drawn to the rich pastures of cumulative years,

As youth pales
My shadow flows through browning pastures
Where grayed stallions with slowed gaits
Feed on the sweet and bitter seeds of the past,
Filled with wisdom of living life.

I live in the paradox of life.

Sources

Gibran, Kahlil. *The Prophet*. New York: Alfred A. Knopf, 1985, p. 29.

Goens, George. "Generations: A Daughter's Death, and a Quest for Answers," *New York Times*, February 18, 2007.

Harrold, Joan K. and Joanne Lynn (eds.) Chinese proverb. *A Good Dying: Shaping Health Care for the Last Months of Life*. New York: Haworth Press, 1998, p. 20.

Kenyon, Jane. "Otherwise," *Otherwise*. St. Paul: Graywolf Press, 1996.

Metaxas, Eric. *Bonhoeffer: Pastor, Martyr, Prophet, Spy*. New York: Thomas Nelson, 2011, pp.105 and 176-7.

Moyers, Bill. *The Language of Life*. New York: Broadway Books, 1995.

O'Donahue, John. *Anam Cara*. New York: Harper Collins, 1998, p. 242.

"Shall We Gather by the River," a traditional Christian hymn written in 1864 by American poet and gospel music composer Robert Lowry.

"Simple Gifts" is a Shaker song written and composed in 1848 by Elder Joseph Brackett.

Tolstoy, Leo. *Childhood, Boyhood, Youth*. New York: Scribner, 1852, 1904.

Wiesel, Elie, with Irving Abrahamson. *Against Silence: The Voice and Vision of Elie Wiesel, Volume 2.* New York: Knopf Publishing Group, 1985, p. 253.

Wood, Nancy. "Native Blessing," *Spirit Walker.* New York: Doubleday Books, 1993.

Acknowledgments

When people face tragedy, they often remember different things. The same is true here. This story is told from my perspective and memories—what I remember, what I felt, and how I interpreted events. This is my story of the actual happenings and the journey I experienced in dealing with Betsy's death.

But any journey is never really taken alone. We carry with us those significant people and mentors who helped make us who we are today. Their wisdom reverberates within us, and guides us in good and difficult times. I am thankful for them all.

I am certainly indebted to friends who stood by me in the deepest of grief. Peter and Eileen "on the farm" and Lou, my great friend and business partner, have been a source of support and comfort.

My sister, Betty, and other family members were compassionate and loving, while facing their own sadness. Bill's parents, Bill and Linda, and Bill senior's wife, Stephanie, were always supportive and considerate.

Jennie, my daughter-in-law, was there for me from the day of the fateful call and throughout the journey, caring and loving to this day. I am grateful to Heather and Bill for providing me valuable "grandpa time" with Claire and Luke. Claire and Luke have given me love and happiness which I cherish beyond words.

Betsy's mother, Mary, is a remarkable mother and teacher. Her love and guidance to our children, Betsy and Curtis, was a dominant force which helped shape them into responsible and considerate adults.

Finally, my wife Marilyn has been a stalwart source of loving encouragement, understanding, and support. I am truly blessed.

Thanks to all.